Presented to

_____

By

_____

Date

_____

Occasion

_____

The Master Is Calling

DISCOVERING

THE WONDERS OF

SPIRIT-LED PRAYER

The *Master*
Is Calling

DISCOVERING

THE WONDERS OF

SPIRIT-LED PRAYER

LYNNE HAMMOND

The Master Is Calling:
Discovering the Wonders of Spirit-Led Prayer

ISBN 1-57399-006-X

All scripture is from the Amplified Bible
unless otherwise noted.
Amplified Bible
©1958, 1987
by the Lockman Foundation.

1 2 3 4 5 6 7 8 9 10 11 12 13 14 15

MAC HAMMOND
M I N I S T R I E S
P.O. BOX 29469
MINNEAPOLIS, MN 55429-2946

To my Prayer Leaders and my "Sparkies,"
who always spark me to new depths and new directions
in the wondrous realm of prayer.

CONTENTS

FOREWARD

For some, prayer is a thing they do. For others, prayer is nothing less than life itself. For Lynne Hammond, it's the latter—life is prayer. I'm in a position to know, she's my wife.

I write as a pastor, not as a biased husband, when I say I know of few other people more qualified to write a book about the deep things of prayer. Over the years Lynne has spent countless hours pouring over books by the great men and women of prayer from generations past—books by giants in prayer such as R.A. Torrey, E.M. Bounds, Lillian Yoeman, Andrew Murray and many others.

I've watched as she mined the scriptures for nuggets of truth and precious principles of praying more effectively, more fervently and with more power.

Most importantly, I've observed as she not only studied about prayer, but lived prayer. I know the hours she spends in the prayer closet. I know the many times she's spent the entire night doing the hard, unseen work of the kingdom of God on her knees.

E.M Bounds once wrote:

> "Prayer is no dreary performance, dead and death-dealing, but it is God's enabling act for man, living and life-giving, joy and joy-giving. Prayer is the contact of a living soul with God. In prayer, God stoops to kiss man, to bless man, and to aid man in everything that God can devise or man can need."

I believe this book can help make your prayer life like that. For years, our church has had the privilege of sitting under Lynne's teaching on the many facets of prayer. This book brings you that same opportunity. May it spur you on to greater depths and heights in prayer than you ever imagined possible.

MAC HAMMOND, *Pastor*
LIVING WORD CHRISTIAN CENTER
MINNEAPOLIS, MINNESOTA

Time for a Change

I said you'd be changed in My presence, saith the Lord. If you have not experienced change in your life, if your old ways are still prevailing, if your old man is still in evidence, you have not spent the time with Me that I desire. It isn't a matter of self control or disciplining your flesh with no help from Me, saith God. If you'll spend time in My presence you will be changed. Your pattern of life will be changed. Your old man will begin to pass away. Your new man will begin to rise in the image of My Son. Your life will begin to bear much fruit. The evidence of your walk with Me will change as a result of spending much time in My presence.

If you're having trouble getting rid of an old habit, if you're having trouble with your marriage, if your family relationships aren't changing, you're not spending the time with Me that would enable that change to come to pass. Your desire and the motivation of your heart to walk uprightly before Me is a product of becoming so close to Me that you do not want to bring hurt to Me.

In natural relationships, when you love someone you want to do the right things for them. You don't want to hurt them. Well, as you spend time with Me, saith God, as you spend time in My presence, we'll develop a relationship that is closer than any earthly relationship. It will shape the pattern of your living. You'll want to conform your ways to My Word simply because it's the desire of your heart. Your life will change; but it will be a product of your spending time with Me.

Prophecy delivered by Lynne Hammond, 2/7/93

CHAPTER 1

Fellowship: The Foundation of Powerful Prayer

This know also, that in the last days perilous times shall come. For men shall be lovers of their own selves, covetous, boasters, proud, blasphemers, disobedient to parents, unthankful, unholy, Without natural affection, trucebreakers, false accusers, incontinent, fierce, despisers of those that are good, Traitors, heady, highminded, lovers of pleasure more than lovers of God; Having a form of godliness, but denying the power thereof: from such turn away.
(2 Timothy 3:1-5 KJV)

Judging strictly by appearances, it might seem that the Church of the Lord Jesus Christ is doing quite well in the area of prayer these days. Pick up almost any church bulletin in any city and you'll find listed midweek prayer meetings, prayer luncheons, prayer requests, perhaps even a printed prayer for the week.

Walk into any church service and you'll hear at least one prayer—probably two or three—before it's done. Listen in on the conversations of Christians and you'll hear them say, "I need you to pray for me, brother." And, no doubt, you'll hear the same response every time. "Oh, yes. I will, I will."

One would think, with all this talk about prayer, the windows of heaven would be opened wide spilling the blessings of God upon us. Jesus plainly promised that "whatsoever ye shall ask in my name, that will I do, that the Father may be glorified in the Son." So we should be swimming in waves of revival, prosperity, healing and miracles of every sort. Our every conversation should be overflowing with joyful reports of answered prayer. The Church should be bursting forth with such earthshaking evidence of God's mighty delivering power and sinners should be banging on our doors by the thousands begging us to show them the way of salvation.

But clearly, that is not the case.

I do not mean to say we have seen no results from our praying. There have always been glimmers and even lightning strikes of the power and presence of God throughout the earth. There have been praying people and even praying congregations here and there who have moved mountains as they lifted their hearts to God—and every day their numbers are increasing. Yet even so, we must admit that in our day the Church as a whole has not experienced what the Bible has promised would come to us through prayer.

Corporately, we have not seen buildings shake under the power of God as we unite in prayer like the Church did in Acts 4. Individually, we have not been able to speak with absolute certainty the words of the apostle John:

> *And this is the confidence that we have in him, that, if we ask any thing according to his will...we know that we have the petitions that we desired of him.* (1 John 5:14-15 KJV).

As a result, many Christians have allowed prayer to slip from their list of priorities. (One survey reported the average Christian invests less than two minutes a day at it.) Many others have struggled through the disappointments of unanswered prayer, trying to explain away their lack of results with theological arguments. "Well," they say, "perhaps it simply wasn't God's will this time."

But I believe every true Christian knows deep in his heart that despite what the theologians may say, our problem is not that God is saying a loving *No,* to many of our requests. It's that our prayers too often lack the depth that heaven requires. They seem to come from the head not the heart. Instead of being propelled from our spirit toward God with an earnestness and faith that cannot be denied, they often wobble from our uncertain lips and fall helplessly to the floor.

They have a form of godliness, but they deny the power thereof.

In times past, we were fooled by that form. We were like the shopper standing in the department store who sees the mannequin out of the corner of his eye and, thinking for a split second the mannequin is real, the shopper turns to speak to it.

But, praise God, we're not being fooled anymore. We've looked that prayer mannequin square in the face and said, "You're not the real thing!" We've turned our faces toward God and begun crying out as the disciples did two thousand years ago, "Lord, teach us to pray!"

And He is answering us. He is restoring to us not just the principles nor the mechanics, but the very *spirit* of prayer.

I Know Whom I Have Believed

It is that spirit we most desperately need. For although principles and formulas are valuable teaching tools, many times we have focused on them to the exclusion of God Himself. We have unwittingly grieved His tender Spirit by approaching Him almost as if He were a machine instead of a Person. We've followed step-by-step formulas as though by systematically pushing scriptural buttons and pulling spiritual levers, we could get Him to produce the results we desire.

Many of us have even recognized the truth that it takes faith to receive from God, so we've studied the Bible, confessed particular verses over and over, and memorized every key to spiritual success. Yet many times, instead of causing us to flourish in faith and prayer, our endeavors have left us dry and spiritless. Why is that? It is because we can't have real faith just by knowing principles. Real faith comes from knowing the Person behind the principles.

That's why the apostle Paul in his great statement of faith wrote, "I know whom I have believed, and am persuaded that he is able to keep that which I have committed unto him against that day" (2 Timothy 1:12 KJV). Paul didn't say, I know *what* I have believed. He didn't say, I know *the principles and steps* I have believed. He said, *I know the Person of the Lord Jesus Christ.*

Paul knew Jesus because he fellowshipped with Him. And that fellowship gave Paul an unshakable confidence in His Word.

Faith and fellowship with God are inseparable!

Notice I said fellowship—not relationship. They're not one and the same. A man and a woman could walk down an aisle, have a minister marry them and legally, they'd have a relationship. Even if they never spoke another word to each other, they would be related by law as husband and wife.

But does that mean they know each other? Does it mean they have fellowship? *No.*

By the same token, every person who has been born again has a relationship with God. But *not* everyone who's been born again has fellowship with Him. A great many people come to the altar, shake hands with Jesus and say, "I receive You as my Savior." He welcomes them to the family and there the fellowship stops.

That kind of experience does not bring eternal life. It will get us to heaven when we die but it will not bring forth the *Zoe,* prayer-inspiring God-kind of life that Jesus intended for us to have.

What *will* produce that quality of life? Jesus tells us in John 17:3. There He says, "And this is life eternal, that they might know thee, the only true God, and Jesus Christ, whom thou hast sent." Eternal life comes from knowing God.

Some will say, "I know God because I know His Word." But let me tell you, it is possible to know the Book backward and forward and still not know the Author. That was true of the Pharisees in Jesus' day. They knew the scriptures thoroughly, yet Jesus said to them:

> *The Father Who sent Me has Himself testified concerning Me. Not one of you has ever given ear to His voice or seen His form (His face— what He is like). [You have always been deaf to His voice and blind to the vision of Him.] And you have not His word (His thought) liv-ing in your hearts, because you do not believe and adhere to and trust in and rely on Him Whom He has sent. [That is why you do not keep His message living in you, because you do not believe in the Messenger Whom He has sent.] You search and investigate and pour over the Scriptures diligently, because you sup-pose and trust that you have eternal life through them. And these [very Scriptures] testify about Me! And still you are not willing [but refuse] to come to Me, so that you might have life.*
> (John 5:37-40)

Please understand, I am a Word person. I love the Word of God. But if you try to apply that Word without fel-lowshipping with the Person and Spirit of God Himself, your

life and your prayers will be dry and powerless. That's
because it is the Holy Spirit who quickens the Word to you.
It's God Himself—the Person and power behind the Word—
Who makes it come alive in your life.

His Presence Makes the Difference

You can see that truth borne out in the lives of Old
Testament heroes, Caleb and Joshua. They were sent out
along with 10 other leaders of the nation of Israel as spies to
scout out the Promised Land.

If you'll read through the book of Exodus, you'll find
God spoke many times to the Israelites saying, "I've given
you this Promised Land. It's a land flowing with milk and
honey. I'll deliver all its people into your hands." Every single
Israelite had heard that promise from God again and again.
Yet when the 12 spies were sent into the land, ten of them
came back with an evil report. They said:

> *We came to the land to which you sent us;*
> *surely it flows with milk and honey...[But it is]*
> *a land that devours its inhabitants. And all the*
> *people that we saw in it are men of great*
> *stature...and we were in our own sight as*
> *grasshoppers, and so we were in their sight.*
> (Numbers 13:27, 32-33)

Joshua and Caleb, on the other hand, had an entirely
different perspective. They brought words of encouragement, saying:

> *Let us go up at once and possess it; we are well*
> *able to conquer it...If the Lord delights in us,*
> *then He will bring us into this land and give it*
> *to us, a land flowing with milk and honey.*
> *Only do not rebel against the Lord, neither fear*
> *the people of the land, for they are bread for us.*
> *Their defense and the shadow [of protection] is*

removed from over them, but the Lord is with
us. Fear them not. (Numbers 13:30, 14:8-9)

What made the difference? All 12 leaders had heard
the Word of the Lord. All of them knew His promise. All of
them had the same potential and the same opportunities.
Why then did Joshua and Caleb have faith in God's promise
while the others didn't?

You can find the answer to that question by looking at
an event that took place earlier in Joshua's life when the
Israelites had just come out of Egypt. At that time:

Moses used to take [his own] tent and pitch it
outside the camp, far off from the camp, and
he called it the tent of meeting [of God with
His own people]. And everyone who sought the
Lord went out to [that temporary] tent of meet-
ing which was outside the camp. When Moses
went out to the tent of meeting, all the people
rose and stood, every man at his tent door,
and looked after Moses until he had gone into
the tent. When Moses entered the tent, the pil-
lar of cloud would descend and stand at the
door of the tent, and the Lord would talk with
Moses. And all the people saw the pillar of
cloud stand at the tent door, and all the people
rose up and worshipped, every man at his tent
door. And the Lord spoke to Moses face to face,
as a man speaks to his friend. Moses returned
to the camp, but his minister Joshua son of
Nun, a young man, did not depart from the
[temporary prayer] tent. (Exodus 33:7-11)

Think of that! Joshua was so hungry for God, he
wouldn't leave the prayer tent! As a result, he not only
heard God's Words, he knew and experienced God's
presence. That's why he was so bold and full of faith

even when confronted with the giants of Canaan.

The same was true with Caleb. God said Caleb had a different spirit from the other ten leaders. He followed God fully (Numbers 14:24).

Caleb and Joshua sought God. They were hungry for Him. They didn't just follow after His blessings. They didn't just hunger after His promises. They wanted *Him.*

The apostle Paul was the same way. He said:

> *[For my determined purpose is] that I may*
> *know Him [that I may progressively become*
> *more deeply and intimately acquainted with*
> *Him, perceiving and recognizing and under-*
> *standing the wonders of His Person more*
> *strongly and more clearly]...* (Philippians 3:10)

That attitude and purpose is the very foundation of vibrant, powerful prayer. Without it, even the most mechanically correct, properly principled prayers will be little more than straws in the wind.

For it is not just the mouth and mind that prays. It is our life that prays. If that life is not the eternal, God-kind of life that springs forth from a heartfelt desire to know Jesus, our prayers will lack force and substance. They will not be "The earnest (heartfelt, continued) prayer of a righteous man (that) makes tremendous power available [dynamic in its working]." (James 5:16)

When Deep Calls to Deep

Real praying comes from the heart hungry for God. It comes when we say, like David did in Psalm 42, "As the hart pants and longs for the water brooks, so I pant and long for You, O God. My inner self thirsts for God, for the living God...[Roaring] deep calls to [roaring] deep at the thunder of Your waterspouts; all Your breakers and Your rolling waves have gone over me."(verses 1-2, 7).

When a person is hungry, the deepest part of his

spirit begins to call out to God for something to fill that hunger. He might not even know what it is he is calling for, but God knows, and this cry touches the depths of His heart and causes Him to respond.

That's how I received the baptism of the Holy Spirit. At the time, I didn't even know what the baptism of the Holy Spirit was. I had been born again only a short time and I'd never even heard of speaking in tongues. I knew nothing of the glory and manifest presence of God.

Even so, my heart was yearning after God. I wanted to know Him. I longed to be able to fellowship with Him and pray. My heart cried, my soul sobbed, my spirit wept for God. But I had no idea what to do about it.

I would pray as far as I could with my understanding, but when I had said all I knew to say to Him, I could still feel my heart reaching out for more. It was so frustrating to me. All I could say was, "God, help me!"

Day after day, the deep in me cried out to Him. Yet instead of easing my hunger, it seemed the more I cried out the greater my longing became. Finally one March night in 1972, it grew so strong I couldn't sleep. I climbed out of bed, wrapped my bathrobe around me and went into the den. Once again, I cried out, "Help me, God. I'm just so hungry for You. I just want to know You. I want to be able to talk to You. Please, help me pray."

Falling into a chair, I began to sob. Then suddenly the power of God flooded the room. The deep in Him answered the deep in me and His presence shook me with great and overwhelming waves of glory. The fire of God fell on me until it felt as though my very skin was on fire.

It was then this beautiful language I didn't know started flowing like a river from within me. I was startled since I had never heard anything about speaking in tongues. Yet the joy of the Lord so filled my soul, I knew this had to be from God.

In the years since, I've looked back on that experience and wondered about it. "Lord," I've asked, "why did You fill me that night?"

"Because you were calling out for it," He answered. "You were hungry for it. And you get whatever you're hungry for."

Spiritual hunger is an interesting thing, however. It's never really satisfied. The more of God you get, the more of Him you want. We can never live on past experiences. We're always needing fresh manna from heaven. So it wasn't long after God gloriously baptized me in His Spirit that I was seeking Him again. It wasn't long before I was crying out, "Lord, please reveal Yourself to me more fully. Speak to my heart!"

Again, He answered in His sweet, wonderful way and said, "Lynne, I am the God of the Book. I'll speak to you from the Book."

Do you think I left my Bible sitting idly on my nightstand after I heard that? No, indeed! I read it...and read it...and read it. Sure enough, He started revealing Himself to me. He revealed Himself as the God Who created the heavens and the earth. He revealed Himself as the God Who split the Red Sea. He revealed Himself as the God who rained manna down from heaven for His children, and healed the blind, the halt and the maimed. He revealed Himself through the life of Jesus and through the signs and wonders of Acts.

That was more than 20 years ago and I'm still reading today. He's still revealing Himself. I know Him far more intimately than I did when I began my life in Him. Yet I'm hungrier now than ever.

Lord, Make Us Hungrier Still

If we want true power in prayer, we must cultivate that kind of hunger. We must let the deep within us begin to call out to the deep in God. We must desire to know Jesus with such an intensity that every other desire pales beside it.

I once read an account of a prayer meeting that took place among some old-time saints of God in the early 1900's. Among those in attendance was a woman named Lillian Thistleweight. She was a great evangelist in her day and her sole cry, all of her hunger, was for the holiness of God.

As she began to talk about her thirst for a sanctified life, she caught the attention of one man in particular. Although he was a Christian man who revered God, he was, by his own account, quite self-satisfied. He was happy, successful and had little desire for anything more. Yet he saw in that saintly woman a quality that stirred his spirit.

As he listened to her speak, he was so overwhelmed with spiritual hunger, with a desire to have that which she possessed in God, he fell to his knees and began to pray. He prayed until the rafters shook. He prayed until it seemed that lighting flashed through the souls of everyone in the room. He prayed until the power of God came down, sanctified every life there and in an instant changed them forever.

That's what real spiritual hunger will do.

It's no wonder that Jesus said, "Blessed are the poor in spirit: for theirs is the kingdom of heaven. Blessed are they which do hunger and thirst after righteousness: for they shall be filled" (Matthew 5:3,6). People who are poor and hungry have only one quest in life. It is to find food. Their entire existence centers around that search for provision. They look...and look...and look for it.

I am convinced it is the lack of spiritual hunger that is at the root of our powerlessness in prayer. It is not that we do not know the rules or principles of prayer. It is not that we haven't had enough instruction on the mechanics of it. It is that we have been so full of ourselves and our own interests that we've left little room for God to move.

Even though we have been born again and baptized in the Holy Spirit, in many ways we need to hear the same words Paul wrote to the Ephesian church. We need someone to say to us, *Awake, O sleeper, and arise from the dead!*

Those seem like strange words for Paul to say to Christians—especially when you consider the church at Ephesus possessed more spiritual knowledge than any other church of its day. Why did they need such a wake-up call?

Revelation 2:4-5 tells us.

> *But I have this [one charge to make] against you:*
> *that you have left (abandoned) the love that you*
> *had at first [you have deserted Me, your first*
> *love.] Remember then from what heights you*
> *have fallen. Repent...or else I will visit you and*
> *remove your lampstand from its place...*

The lampstand in that scripture is a symbol of the Holy Spirit. The Holy Spirit is the source of our power. He brings the anointing. But if we allow our passion for Jesus to grow cold, even though we may once have been filled with the Holy Spirit's fire, we will lose our power—in life and in prayer.

That's why the Bible tells us not to be filled with the Holy Spirit just once, but to be *ever filled and stimulated by Him* (Ephesians 5:18). The original Greek literally says we are to *be being filled with the Spirit!*

We must maintain the life of God within us. And we can't do it simply by going to church a couple of times a week. We can't do it by fellowshipping with God only at public gatherings of believers. We need to have a love affair with the Lord—and love affairs are never in public!

God is calling us to cultivate a relationship with Him where we fellowship with Him constantly, all day long. He not only wants us to bring our needs and desires and petitions before Him, but to live daily in union and communion with Him.

Above All: Abide in Him

Those times of daily communion, those times of waiting before God and worshipping Him are what bring forth a vibrant prayer life. It's not just checking in with Him now and then, but abiding constantly in Him that gives us His power. That's why Jesus gave us these instructions in John 15:

Dwell in Me, and I will dwell in you. [Live in Me, and I will live in you.] Just as no branch can bear fruit of itself without abiding in (being vitally united to) the vine, neither can you bear fruit unless you abide in Me. I am the vine; you are the branches. Whoever lives in Me and I in him bears much (abundant) fruit. However, apart from Me [cut off from vital union with Me] you can do nothing. If a person does not dwell in Me, he is thrown out like a [broken-off] branch, and withers; such branches are gathered up and thrown into the fire, and they are burned. If you live in Me [abide vitally united to Me] and My words remain in you and continue to live in your hearts, ask whatever you will, and it shall be done for you. (verscs 4-7)

The word *ask* in that last verse has a far deeper meaning than most people realize. It implies you and God are so intertwined, your life and His life so closely joined together that when you ask Him something, it's not really just you asking—it's Him asking too.

Once you begin abiding in Jesus, once you grow accustomed to having daily times of communion with Him, you'll find you cannot live without them. You'll find yourself so craving to be in His manifest presence you can hardly wait to get into your place of prayer. Instead of hurrying to finish your time with God so you can get on with the rest of your day as you once did, you'll hurry through everything else so you can have more precious time with Him.

Daily prayer promotes devotion to God. It keeps Him in the center of your heart. It causes you to be most wonderfully addicted to His presence so that the more you know Him, the more of Him you want to know.

Why then do so few Christians spend this daily time in fellowship with God?

In many cases it's because they've been taught that prayer is a duty rather than a delight. So, when they have made an effort to have a daily prayer time, they've approached it with a sense of drudgery. They go to prayer with cold hearts bent on satisfying a religious requirement rather than with hearts warmed by expectation, eagerly anticipating a time of fellowship with their Father. They do not draw genuinely near to God; therefore, He does not draw near to them. So they soon lose interest in the ritual and cast it aside.

Those who do begin to discover the wonders of daily communion with God inevitably run into other difficulties—the Devil, for instance. He is so frightened of the Christian who abides in God that he will go to great lengths to interfere with those times of fellowship. He will see to it that interruptions, distractions, schedule conflicts arise until it seems almost impossible to find a quiet time and place for prayer.

I remember one summer in my life when that was particularly true. We were remodeling our home, so Mac and I had to sleep on the sofa bed in the den. We also had guests and I can remember waking up some mornings with eight people already walking around in my house. There seemed to be nowhere to get alone with God.

"Lord," I said in desperation, "I need a plan!" Sure enough, He gave me an idea. I would back the car out of the garage and park it in the driveway. Then I'd lie down in the back seat and pray. No one knew where I was, so no one interrupted me.

Some people might think that's strange. But I can tell you, if you want to have this wonderful intimacy with God you must be so determined that you don't mind being a little strange every once in a while. You must be willing to lay aside all the natural things that scream for your attention and do whatever it takes to make your time with Him your number one priority.

I often say, "I don't care if the church members are

fighting on the lawn; I don't care if the President of the United States calls; don't disturb me when I'm in prayer. It's the most important thing in my life!'"

Praying With the Power of Elijah

Someone might say, "Well, Sister Hammond, you're that way because you're in the ministry."

No, I'm not! I'm that way because I'm a Christian. This isn't some kind of lofty, super-spiritual life we're talking about here. This is just basic, bottom-line Christianity. This is the Christianity the Bible describes.

The Bible doesn't paint a picture of Christians who only pray every once in a while. It doesn't depict us as people who get answers to prayer on occasion. The Bible says we're *constant in prayer* (Romans 12:12). And as to the effectiveness of those prayers, it says in James 5:16-18:

> *Pray...for one another, that you may be
> healed... The earnest (heartfelt, continued)
> prayer of a righteous man makes tremendous
> power available [dynamic in its working].
> Elijah was a human being with a nature such
> as we have [with feelings, affections, and a con-
> stitution like ours]: and he prayed earnestly for
> it not to rain, and no rain fell on the earth for
> three years and six months. And [then] he
> prayed again and the heavens supplied rain
> and the land produced its crops...*

Am I saying God expects us to pray with the power of Elijah? No, the *Bible* is saying that! It says he was a human being just like we are. He had all the same struggles and natural weaknesses we have.

He is not set forth as an unusual fellow who lived off in the spiritual stratosphere somewhere. He is given to us as an inspiration and an example of earnest praying. And if there's anything this generation and this world needs right now *it is earnest praying.*

We've had enough superficial performances of prayer. We've had enough spiritless, weak praying. Now we need prayers that avail with God so powerfully they can change the course of nature; prayer that changes people and nations; prayer that projects God in full force to the world.

That's what Elijah's prayer did.

One translation says of Elijah, "with prayer, he prayed." In other words, he prayed with all of the combined energies and forces of God. How was he able to do that?

Read 1 Kings 17 and you'll find out. There we see Elijah coming boldly before Ahab, the wicked king of Israel, announcing, "As the Lord, the God of Israel, lives, before Whom I stand, there shall not be dew or rain these years but according to My word." (1 Kings 17:1).

Notice Elijah didn't just meander around. He didn't say, "Well, you know, I feel kind of impressed that it might be the Lord's will for rain to not fall around here for a while." No, he was firm and clear. He said, "Here's how it will be. Absolutely. Period. End of conversation." He reveals the reason for his confidence and power in the phrase *the Lord God of Israel,* **before Whom I stand**.

That was the secret of Elijah's praying. He had stood in the power and presence of God. He didn't just make up those words he spoke to Ahab on his own. He had received them from God Himself. In the times of fellowship like those he spent beside the brook Cherith alone with God, Elijah had come again and again before Him in prayer and because he had stood in that place, he could speak and pray with world-shaking authority.

You and I have a far greater covenant than Elijah did. Through the precious blood of Jesus, God has opened for us a new and living Way so that we can come boldly before the throne of grace to obtain mercy and find grace to help in time of need (Hebrews 4:16). He has given us a freedom of access to Him the Old Testament saints never knew. He's made available to us all the resources and power of heaven.

But what have we done with those privileges? For the most part, we've done very little. We've been too busy making a living, or watching television, or perhaps even participating in church activities to take advantage of them. As a Church, we have pacified our spiritual hunger with the junk food the world has offered us while we let the dust collect on our Bible and the cobwebs grow in our prayer closets.

Right now you may be thinking, *Yes, it's true. I have done that in the past but I want to change it now. What can I do?*

Simply repent before God. Honestly acknowledge that you have desired other things more than Him. You cannot pretend to be hungry when you are not. But you can begin to call out to Him and say, "Lord, please forgive me and make me hungry for You."

You can from this day on, say as David did, "Your face, Lord I will seek" (Psalms 27:8, NIV). Set aside time to fellowship with God in prayer and in the Word every day, not out of a sense of religious duty but because you want to whet your spiritual appetite and you know the fragrance of His presence as you meet Him daily in some quiet place, will stir the hunger in your heart. It will awaken the craving that sleeps within every true child of God. It will remind you of how empty you are without Him and cause you to cry out from the depths of your soul, "Lord, I want to know You!"

In the natural course of this earth wherever there's a vacuum, that vacuum causes the air to rush in and fill its emptiness. Thus, the wind blows there. The same is true in the spirit realm. If we'll empty ourselves of the distractions and desires of this world, and crave Jesus alone—He will rush into our lives with the wind of the Holy Spirit. He will meet us with an intensity and an outpouring we have, until now, only read about in the pages of books.

We will know not just the form of prayer... but its power.

CHAPTER 2

Praying From Your Heart

*he foreigners who join themselves to the
Lord to minister to Him and to love the name
of the Lord and to be His servants, everyone
who keeps the Sabbath so as not to profane it
and who holds fast My covenant [by conscien-
tious obedience]—all these I will bring to My
holy mountain and make them joyful in My
house of prayer. Their burnt offerings and
their sacrifices will be accepted on My altar;
for My house will be called a house of prayer
for all peoples.* (Isaiah 56:6-7)

One of the reasons the Church has had such great difficulty in prayer is we've made it more complicated than it
is. We have surrounded it with religious rules and regula-
tions and regarded it as so spiritually lofty as to be almost
unobtainable to the average Christian.

But actually, prayer is quite simple. It is nothing more
nor less than communication with God. And if you're a
born-again believer, prayer is as natural to you spiritually

as breathing is to you physically. Your spirit by its very nature cries out spontaneously to God, "Abba, Father" (See Romans 8:15).

In fact, prayer is who you are, not just something you do. Read Isaiah 56:7 and you can see what I mean. There the Lord said, "My house will be called a house of prayer." In old covenant times, God's house was a building, a temple built in His honor. But today, we're under the new covenant and God no longer lives in a temple of stone. He inhabits the spirits of born-again men and women. As 1 Corinthians 3:16 KJV says, "Know ye not that ye are the temple of God, and that the Spirit of God dwelleth in you?"

The house of prayer isn't the church building down the block. It isn't some sanctuary somewhere. *You* are God's house of prayer!

Once you realize that, you can stop straining at it. You can quit trying to manufacture elegant, super-spiritual-sounding phrases and simply start expressing your heart to God. Instead of trying to construct the perfect prayer, you can just be honest and open with Him.

"But I don't know how to do that!" you may say. "Every time I try to pray, I freeze up. It's as if I hit a brick wall."

Then tell God about it! Say, "Father, I want to talk to You. But I seem to be hitting a brick wall and I'm not able to express myself. I don't know what to do about it, Lord. So I'm just asking You to help me."

It sounds almost childishly simple, doesn't it? Yet the truth is, a prayer like that spoken from the heart will produce far greater results than the grandest prayer designed by the mind of man. That's because it's the *heartfelt prayer* (James 5:16) not the *headfelt prayer* that makes tremendous power available.

Effective praying comes from your heart, not your head. Not one time does the Word of God tell us to pray from our minds. It says we're to pray from our hearts. Even when you "pray with your understanding" (1 Corinthians 14:15), you should still be praying from your heart.

If you've spent more time and effort developing your mind or your intellect than your spirit, you may have difficulty locating your heart at first. But you can solve that problem by spending more time in the Word of God. For Hebrews 4:12 KJV says, "...the word of God is quick, and powerful, and sharper than any two-edged sword, piercing even to the dividing asunder of soul and Spirit, and of the joints and marrow, and is a discerner of the thoughts and intents of the heart."

As you read and meditate the Word, it will help you distinguish between your heart and your head. It will help you cultivate your sensitivity to the Spirit. That sensitivity is very important in prayer because you are a spirit and God is a spirit; so the way you contact Him is from spirit to spirit, from heart to heart!

Getting Honest With God

In 1 Samuel, you can find an example of just how wonderfully effective prayer can be when it comes honestly and openly from the depths of your heart. Chapter one tells about Hannah, a woman who was deeply grieved by her inability to bear a child. Adding to her sorrow was the fact that her husband had another wife who could bear children and who provoked Hannah by mocking her barren condition. As a result, Hannah became so distressed that she wept and did not eat.

Although Hannah's barrenness was physical, I've seen spiritual barrenness have the same effect on people. I've seen people with a desperation to know God and be fruitful in prayer that surpasses even their hunger for physical food. I've seen them so intensely desire to have the will of God done in their lives it causes them to weep.

In Hannah's case, Elkanah her husband said to her, "Hannah, why weepest thou? and why eatest thou not? and why is thy heart grieved? am not I better to thee than ten sons?" (1:8 KJV). He loved her greatly and tried to fill up this void in her life, but he couldn't.

That's the way it is in spiritual things too. It doesn't matter how wonderful people are to you, they cannot satisfy the deep, inner desire you have to know God's plan for your life. They can't fill the longing you have for fellowship with your heavenly Father.

Eventually, Hannah's distress grew so great, she went to the temple of the Lord:

> *And she was in bitterness of soul, and prayed unto the Lord, and wept sore. And she vowed a vow, and said, O Lord of hosts, if thou wilt indeed look on the affliction of thine handmaid, and remember me, and not forget thine handmaid, but wilt give unto thine handmaid a man child, then I will give him unto the Lord all the days of his life, and there shall no razor come upon his head. And it came to pass, as she continued praying before the Lord, that Eli [the priest] marked her mouth. Now Hannah, she spake in her heart; only her lips moved, but her voice was not heard: therefore Eli thought she had been drunken. And Eli said unto her, How long wilt thou be drunken? put away thy wine from thee. And Hannah answered and said, No, my lord, I am a woman of a sorrowful spirit: I have drunk neither wine nor strong drink, but have poured out my soul before the Lord...Then Eli answered and said, Go in peace: and the God of Israel grant thee thy petition that thou hast asked of him. And she said, Let thine handmaid find grace in thy sight. So the woman went her way, and did eat, and her countenance was no more sad.* (verses 10-18 KJV)

If you'll read the rest of the story, you'll find God not only gave Hannah the son she requested, He gave her five other children as well. How did she get such remarkable results? Did she obtain them by mechanically applying a formula for answered prayer? Did she get them by working up the best, most wonderful-sounding petition she possibly could?

No, she did it by pouring out her heart honestly and openly to God and by believing He heard and answered her prayer just as the priest said He would.

Clean Out the Clutter

If you're sensing a barrenness in your prayer life, you may need to do the same thing. You may need to do as Lamentations 2:19 says and "Arise [from your bed], cry out in the night, at the beginning of the watches; pour out your heart like water before the face of the Lord."

You see, your soul is like a container. It has many things inside it. Most people just try to relate to God from the surface of that container, so their relationship with Him remains very superficial.

Those people remind me of a teacher I had in seventh grade. She was an extremely unique person and one of the most memorable things about her was the closet in her classroom. She packed it so full she couldn't open the door all the way because if she did, a mountain of stuff would come tumbling down upon her. Whenever she brought a coat to school, she would open the closet just a crack, jam the coat inside and slam the door!

Some people's souls are like that. They're cluttered up with spiritual debris and emotional junk they've accumulated over the years. What they need to do is open the door to their hearts and let everything just fall out before the Lord.

In other words, they need to get very honest before God.

Actually, we all need to do that. We need to stop trying to present to God our spiritual side, the part of us that's all brushed up nice and neat. We need to be real and admit to God we have problems with our attitudes and motivations and ask Him to come in and change them.

Did you know you can keep God out of certain areas of your life by refusing to expose them to Him? You can close the door on Him by failing to communicate with Him honestly about them and trying to act like something you're not.

By the same token, you can throw open that door with simple honesty in prayer by saying, "God, did You know what I thought this morning? It was the most ghastly thing! I need you to forgive me and help me in that area."

Pouring out your soul is like cleaning out that cluttered closet. Some things just need to be confessed, put under the blood of Jesus and thrown away forever. Other things—cares and worries—need to be given to God in faith. Still other issues may just need to be discussed with the Lord, then put back in your heart in a more orderly fashion.

You may even discover some things within you that are too big to articulate in words. You can sense them in there, but you don't know exactly what they are—much less how to communicate them. In those instances, you can pour them out to the Lord in other tongues. You may even find yourself weeping as you do that. If so, just yield to that weeping because it is the Holy Spirit moving upon you. Keep praying until you feel the peace of God and sense that you have finished pouring out your heart.

If your "closet" hasn't been cleaned out for a while, it may take you more than one prayer session to reach that sense of completion. If so, that's fine, set aside time each day and keep going back to the Lord until, with the help of the Holy Spirit, you get the job done.

From then on, keep your soul uncluttered by communicating to the Lord often—honestly, openly and always straight from the heart.

CHAPTER 3

Learning to Flow With the Holy Ghost

But the Comforter, which is the Holy Ghost, whom the Father will send in my name, he shall teach you all things...(John 14:26 KJV)

If you are accustomed to following rigidly prescribed formulas for prayer, right now you may be wondering how you will ever learn to pray from your heart. With no preset outline or steps to guide, how can you be sure you're getting it right?

Don't worry about it! You don't have to figure it out on your own, you have the Holy Spirit to teach you. He can do it very well too. I can testify to that personally.

When I first began my prayer life in 1973 as a new believer, freshly baptized with the Holy Spirit, I had no teaching on the subject at all. Although I began to sense the moving of the Spirit within me directing me to pray, I didn't always yield to Him.

One day I was being particularly disobedient in that

area. All day long, I had a burden to pray for a specific group of people and I knew it. But instead of taking the time to pray, I just went about my business.

That night, the promptings continued. I would wake up for a few minutes with the sense I needed to pray for those people, but instead of yielding, I'd go back to sleep. The next morning, the people called me about their situation and asked if I would pray for them. They had a dire need and I regretted not praying earlier as the Lord had prompted me to do.

On that very day, Jesus Himself came to my bedroom, pointed His finger at me and said these words, "Just as I have written on the stones the commandment of the Lord, so I am this day writing the commandment of the Lord upon your heart and it is this: This house shall be called a house of prayer."

At that time, I was so unfamiliar with the Bible I didn't know God had written the ten commandments with His finger on tablets of stone. I didn't know the book of Isaiah said, "My house shall be called a house of prayer." But I did know that, for days afterward, my heart burned as if on fire.

I knew I had received a mandate from the Lord, yet I was completely ignorant about how to fulfill it. I'd never heard of things like intercession or travailing in prayer. There were no tapes or seminars on prayer like there are today. The only resource I had, other than the Bible and the Holy Spirit, was a denominational church and a well-meaning minister so untaught in the things of the Spirit that when I told Him I'd received the baptism of the Holy Ghost, he gave me a book on exorcism!

There was only one solution. I said, "Lord, I don't know how to do this. So You'll just have to teach me."

I didn't say it just once, either. I said it over and over again.

As a result, I discovered something that absolutely changed my life forever. I discovered that what 1 John 2:27 KJV says is true.

*But the anointing which ye have received of
(God) abideth in you, and ye need not that
any man teach you: but as the same anointing teacheth you of all things, and is truth,
and is no lie, and even as it hath taught
you, ye shall abide in him.*

Day after day, as I trusted the Lord to help me, I found
the Holy Spirit would put promptings in my heart to let me
know how to pray. His anointing within me would lead me
in prayer and teach me all I needed to know if I would only
yield to it.

So that's how I learned to pray—not by memorizing
formulas or following outlines but by following those
promptings of the Spirit.

Every time I started to pray I would check my heart.
When I say check my heart, I mean I would look within
myself (because that's where the Holy Spirit dwells) to see
what God was leading me to pray for. Sometimes those leadings were ever so slight, but I found as I followed them, the
Lord would strengthen them and help me to pray them out
even when I didn't understand them mentally.

In those early days as I was just learning these things,
some of His promptings seemed ever so strange to me.
There was one instance in particular in 1974 when I kept
seeing (not with my physical eyes, of course, but inside in
my spirit) the image of a man with his fingers crushed. It was
a terrible sight and every time I saw it I thought, "Lord, what
is that?"Yet the Lord did not reveal to me who he was. So, I'd
simply pray for him, trusting the Lord to take care of the situation—whatever it might be.

Months later, a man who worked at my husband's
place of business was run over by a piece of machinery and,
sure enough, his fingers were crushed. The first report was
that he would lose his hands but he didn't. In fact, it turned
out that his hands were just fine. When I heard about that
incident, the Holy Spirit quickened my heart, reminding me

of those prayers and I knew then, that man was the one for whom I'd been praying.

Often when I tell about those early days in my prayer life, people ask me how I knew the promptings came from my heart and weren't just imaginations from my mind. The only answer I have is that I simply knew. The Holy Spirit taught me just like He will teach you.

I will note, however, that I spent a great deal of time reading and meditating on the Word of God. And the more I did that, the more easily I could tell when some prompting or thought was not from God. I could discern the difference between my mind and my heart because the Word was helping me divide the two.

Why Use a List When You Have the Holy Ghost?

As the years passed, I began to run across various prayer teachings. Some of those teachings took scriptural principles and turned them into outlines and formulas for prayer. Others suggested you use a prayer list that you make up by sitting down and trying to think of everything and everyone that needs prayer.

Always eager to improve my prayer life, at times I would try to implement those formulas, but whenever I did, I found my prayer times drying up, becoming duty and drudgery. What's more, praying by formula didn't seem to work. When I prayed from a prayer list, for example, I found that if I wrote neatly on a page all the things I wanted to pray about and numbered them, say, from 1 to 25, the first item on the list always got the most prayer.

I'd really go after number one! I'd say, "Lord, I just lift this person up to You. Father, help them to finish the course You've prepared for them. Give them wisdom and revelation. Strengthen them with Your might and direct their steps, keeping them in Your perfect will..." et cetera. The second person on the list would get a little less prayer. Item number three received even less attention. By the time I reached number five, I'd just slap my hand down on the list and say, "Bless them all, Lord. Amen!"

Even if I started in the middle of the list, number 25 never got any prayer. I would think, *This isn't right!* So I would go back to praying by the leading of the Spirit. I would go back to following my heart. Eventually, I didn't even try any of those other methods of prayer because I found that when I prayed by yielding to the Spirit, I enjoyed greater manifestations of God's power and presence in my prayer times—and it's His manifest presence that keeps me coming back to prayer. It's His fellowship that makes prayer such a delight.

That's not just true in my life, either. That's true for every Christian. Every born-again believer has a desire to let communication flow from their heart to God.

I remember one woman said to me, "You know, when I first began my relationship with the Lord, I had the most wonderful times in prayer. I would just talk to God so easily and we would fellowship and enjoy each other. But after a while I got some teaching. I started learning how to regiment my prayer life and put all the different kinds of prayer in little boxes so everything could be all neat and tidy. When I did that, I lost the joy of communion with God and I began to pray less and less. Finally, I just decided to go back to that relationship I had with Him in the beginning. And when I did, I rediscovered my love for prayer."

The truth is, praying by the unction of the Holy Spirit is the only Biblical way to pray. How else are you going to obey the scriptural instruction given in Ephesians 6:18 to pray for all saints? When the Bible says all saints, it means *all* saints!

The first time I read that verse I thought to myself, *How am I going to pray for all saints if I don't know all saints?* I figured I could probably make up a list of about 1,000 and I might be able to cover that list in a month if I prayed very fast. But that's still not praying for all saints.

Then one day it came to me like a flash: *If I'm going to pray for all saints I will have to have the help of the Holy*

Ghost! He knows them all. He knows who needs to be prayed for right now. And He knows exactly what to pray. Why would I resort to using a list when I can be led by Him?

Actually, if you'll read all of Ephesians 6:18 you'll see it specifically tells us that's how we're to pray. It says, "Pray at all times (on every occasion, in every season) in the Spirit, with all [manner of] prayer and entreaty. To that end keep alert and watch with strong purpose and perserverance, interceding in behalf of all the saints (God's consecrated people)."

Notice that verse doesn't instruct us to pray with our heads. It commands us to pray at all times *in the Spirit.* Some people think to pray in the Spirit means to pray in other tongues, but that's not necessarily true. Sometimes tongues are in the Spirit; sometimes they aren't. To pray in the Spirit means to follow the leadership of the Holy Ghost and pray as He directs.

He may direct you to pray in tongues. He may direct you to make supplication for a particular person in a specific way. He may direct you to worship God. He may direct you to bind the Devil. To pray in the Spirit, you must flow with Him.

Let the Rivers Flow!

I've found when I do that, prayer becomes like a river. I have personal experience with rivers because I went kayaking with my husband one summer. I discovered then that rivers are constantly changing. They can be flowing along ever so smoothly one moment, then you round a bend and suddenly the water is a churning rush of rapids. Go around another corner and you'll find the water flows peacefully again.

That's what it's like to pray by the Spirit. It's an adventure. He'll lead you one way for a little while, then He'll take you in a different direction with an entirely different kind of tone. One moment you might just be worshipping quietly, singing to the Lord. Then the Spirit might lead you into a time of weeping and intercession for the lost. But one thing is sure, if you're being led of the Spirit, you won't mistakenly latch onto one kind of prayer and pray that way all the time.

Sometimes sincere people who have a desire to pray make exactly that mistake. They'll see a seasoned person of prayer praying in a particular manner. Perhaps they see him praying loudly and fiercely. So they say to themselves, "That's spiritual. That's the way I'm going to pray."

They may even make a little doctrine out of it and start teaching that fervent effective prayer is always loud and fierce. Of course, nothing is further from the truth. Quiet prayer can be extremely fervent just as loud prayer can be nothing but empty noise. But because people get caught up in forms, they often copy one particular type of prayer they've seen as effective and just camp on it.

Now the problem is this. The seasoned person of prayer prayed in that particular manner at that particular time because they were led by the Holy Spirit to do so. However, the people who copied that kind of prayer were just creating a fleshly imitation. They were "pretending" to do what those seasoned prayers did naturally as a result of their relationship with God.

It reminds me of the times my twin sister and I used to go to my grandmother's house when we were little girls. One of our favorite activities was to play "dress up." We'd put on grandmother's fancy dresses, drape ourselves in costume jewelry from her big jewelry box, perch one of her hats on our heads, then clomp down the street in her high heel shoes. We thought we looked as beautiful as anything you ever could behold and we did not understand why people laughed at us.

That's what it's like when you try to copy someone else's prayer. You're trying to wear clothes that don't fit you. So don't do it. Just locate your own heart. Follow what the Spirit is saying to *you*.

Remember, the Bible says, "All who are led by the Spirit of God [not all who are led by each other!] are sons of God"

(Romans 8:14 KJV). It also instructs us to pray with all kinds of prayer—not just one kind. And the only way you can effectively do that is by learning to flow with the Holy Spirit.

Jesus said in John 7:38-39 KJV, "He that believeth on me, as the scripture hath said, out of his belly shall flow rivers of living water. (...this spake he of the Spirit, which they that believe on him should receive.)"

Notice Jesus said rivers would flow from us. Not just one river. *Rivers!* Those rivers include all kinds of prayer. As you learn to let those rivers flow, you'll find yourself praying the right kind of prayer at just the right time. But you won't be praying it out of your head because somebody told you this is the kind of prayer to pray in this particular situation.

You might as well settle it right now, you'll never be able to pray the right kind of prayer when you're directed by head-knowledge because the Bible says, "We know not what we should pray for as we ought!" (Romans 8:26 KJV) As long as you're praying from your head you'll be praying the wrong thing at the wrong time. You'll be rebuking the Devil when you should be making requests. You'll be worshipping when you should be rebuking the Devil. And as a result, the effectiveness of your prayers will be seriously hindered.

When you let the rivers of the Spirit flow, you'll not only go in the right direction, you'll begin to go deeper into the realms of the spirit. The prophet Ezekiel had a vision of those deeper waters. In Ezekiel 47:1-5 KJV, he wrote:

> *Afterward he brought me again unto the door of the house; and, behold, waters issued out from under the threshold of the house eastward: for the forefront of the house stood toward the east, and the waters came down from under the right side of the house, at the south side of the altar. Then brought he me out of the way of the gate northward...and, behold, there ran out waters on the right side. And when the man*

*that had the line in his hand went forth
eastward, he measured a thousand cubits,
and he brought me through the waters; the
waters were to the ankle. Again he measured a thousand, and brought me through
the waters; the waters were to the knees.
Again he measured a thousand, and
brought me through; the waters were to the
loins. Afterward he measured a thousand;
and it was a river that I could not pass over:
for the waters were risen, waters to swim in,
a river that could not be passed over.*

That's the way Spirit-led prayer progresses. God
doesn't throw you out in the deep waters when you first
begin praying any more than you would put a child who was
just learning to swim in the middle of a river. No, he starts
you off in ankle-deep waters. He leads you first into simple,
honest communications with Him like those we discussed
earlier in this chapter. Then, as you begin to grow in faith and
learn to flow with Him, He'll take you out into those knee-
deep waters.

The more you cultivate your relationship with Him
through prayer and the Word, the more your anointing for
prayer will increase. Eventually, you'll find yourself moving
into places in prayer you never could have imagined when
you first began. You'll have wonderful experiences and
manifestations.

But remember this, you must never seek those experiences and manifestations. You must simply seek the Lord
Himself. Spend time in His Word and in prayer every day.
Then follow Him and yield to promptings He puts in
your heart.

CHAPTER 4

Go for the Gold

O foolish Galatians, who hath bewitched you, that ye should not obey the truth, before whose eyes Jesus Christ hath been evidently set forth, crucified among you? This only would I learn of you, Received ye the Spirit by the works of the law, or by the hearing of faith? Are ye so foolish? having begun in the Spirit, are ye now made perfect by the flesh? (Galatians 3:1-3 KJV)

It's only fair to warn you that even though your heart delights in flowing with the Holy Spirit and being wholly dependent upon Him, your fleshly nature does not. It gravitates toward forms and formulas. It doesn't want to wait on the Lord for His direction, it just pulls you to do something you've done before.

I remember some years ago when I went to lead a particular prayer meeting, my heart was so drawn out to God that the moment I lifted my hands to Him, His power and presence fell upon the room. Those of us who were there could hardly breathe or move because the power of God was so strong.

You probably can guess what I did when I walked into that prayer meeting the next week, can't you? I lifted my hands just like I had the previous week. But this time, the power of God didn't fall upon us. That's because I wasn't lifting my hands as a sincere, Spirit-led expression of my heart to God. I was lifting them because when I had done it before, it had produced the desired result. I was doing it as a fleshly form.

Second Timothy 3:5 warns us about such things. It says they have a form of godliness, but deny its power. A form is anything that doesn't come from your heart. It is a reproduction of something that was once real. As soon as you make something a form, you rob it of its effectiveness.

Our fleshly nature gravitates toward forms because they belong to the sense realm. They can be seen and heard and touched. They can be easily managed and controlled.

That's why the children of Israel sought a form to worship right after God brought them out of Israel. Even though the invisible, almighty God Himself had just delivered them from captivity with astounding signs and wonders, Exodus 32 tells us that as soon as Moses went up the mountain to meet God and left them alone, they went to Aaron and said:

> *...make us gods, which shall go before us... And Aaron said unto them, Break off the golden earrings, which are in the ears of your wives, of your sons, and of your daughters, and bring them unto me. And all the people brake off the golden earrings which were in their ears, and brought them unto Aaron. And he received them at their hand and fashioned it with a graving tool, after he had made it a molten calf: and they said, These be thy gods, O Israel, which brought thee up out of the land of Egypt.* (verses 1-4 KJV)

Do you think the Israelites actually believed the golden calf was the God that brought them out of Egypt? Certainly not! That calf was made out of their jewelry and they knew it. But they wanted a symbol of power. They wanted a form they could worship in a fleshly way.

If you'll read the rest of the story you'll see that God didn't think very highly of such worship. In fact, He called it idolatry.

Today we shake our heads at what the Israelites did. "Weren't they awful?" we say. Then we often turn right around and do the same thing by praying a heartless prayer that has the proper form but lacks power of the Holy Spirit.

Relationship Not Ritual

If you'll keep in mind that God is a person and our prayers to Him are a matter of relationship and not ritual, you can easily see why He doesn't respond to forms. Real prayer is genuine communication. Religious form, however, is a type of manipulation.

Think in terms of a husband and wife for a moment. Imagine a husband walking in one day and putting his arms around his wife, and as a heartfelt expression of love, he says "Honey, you're the most wonderful woman in the world. I'm so glad I married you!"

No doubt, his wife would respond very well to such a communication. She might make his favorite dinner and treat him like a king all night long because he touched her heart with his simple display of affection.

What do you think will happen, however, if the husband says to himself, *Hey, that worked great! I believe I will say that same sentence every night when I get home so she'll do those nice things for me all the time.* The wife won't respond so favorably when the words are said by rote instead of in a spirit of sincerity. After several days of ritualistic repetition, the same sentiments that initially touched her heart would become downright irritating.

Even though most of us would never do such a silly thing in our marriage, we often do it to God without a second thought. We may have learned and experienced the power of the scriptural truths such as "God inhabits the praises of His people (Psalm 22:3). So we begin our prayer times by lifting up our hearts to Him in genuine adoration and worship. Sure enough, His sweet presence manifests and we begin to flow in a river of Spirit-inspired praise.

Then the fleshly nature says, *Aha! I've discovered the formula for getting into God's presence.* So the next time we come to prayer, we start saying words of praise, not because we mean them but because we said them during our last prayer time and they worked. Our heart might be cold as ice but we're saying, "Praise You, Lord. Praise you. Hallalujah. I worship You, Lord." Then we might just speak mindlessly in tongues while our thoughts wander off to make a grocery list or plans the rest of the day.

There is no power in that kind of prayer. It is nothing more than an empty form and God does not respond to it.

How do you avoid slipping into such forms? It's very simple, really. Every time you pray, just determine to reach out honestly to God from your heart. Purpose to make a connection with Him by becoming consciously aware not just that you are speaking—but that you are speaking *to Him.* As James 4:8 says, "Come close to God and He will come close to you."

If your heart seems particularly cold and distant, get out your Bible and stir yourself up by meditating on God's Word. Spend some moments just centering your attention on Him. Instead of letting yourself be preoccupied with what you need, fill your consciousness with thoughts of the mighty and loving Father who has promised to meet those needs.

Before you start flooding the air with your requests, make sure you are truly aware that you have an audience with God and are actually in His presence. Remind your-self that as you talk to God, He is listening. Then purposely believe He is going to grant the things you ask of Him.

I know that sounds quite elementary but it's amaz-ing how many times we fail to do it. As a result, we often end up with little more than an empty imitation of what prayer is truly meant to be.

First Kings 14 tells of a sad time in the history of Israel when a king of Egypt invaded Jerusalem and robbed the temple and the palace of the king.

> *He took away the treasures of the house of*
> *the Lord and of the king's house; he took*
> *away all, including all the shields of gold*
> *which Solomon had made. King Rehoboam*
> *made in their stead bronze shields and com-*
> *mitted them to the hands of the captains of*
> *the guard who kept the door of the king's*
> *house.* (verses 26-27)

How often that has happened to us in prayer! How often we have rushed through it, saying all the right words, doing all the right things, yet only in form and not in substance. How quick we've been to settle for the brass and miss out on the golden treasure of God's manifest presence.

But surely those days are coming to an end. For once believers begin to go for the gold and experience precious power of real prayer, neither the flesh, nor reli-gion, nor the Devil himself will ever again be able to talk them into settling for anything less.

How Long Is Long Enough?

Before I leave the subject of forms, let me specifi-cally mention that almost every time I speak about prayer, people ask me how long they should pray each day. I can't tell you the answer to that question and neither can anyone else because the answer is different for all of us.

We must each do what God is telling us to do about prayer. There is no sacred formula to follow. We must be led by the Spirit in that matter as well.

There was a time in my life when I thought the longer you prayed the more spiritual you were. So I'd pray for two hours, get up off my knees and think, *That isn't enough.* Do you know what changed that for me? I decided to obey the conviction of my own heart.

As I did, I found there were seasons when God might lead me to spend longer times meditating the Word and shorter hours in prayer. Then He'd take me through another season when I'd spend more time in prayer.

What mattered most was not how long I prayed each day, what was important was that I obeyed my heart and did what God was directing me to do right then. There was a time in my life in the early 1970's, for instance, when God first began dealing with me very strongly about prayer and these truths began to come into my heart that the Lord would lead me to read John 15 over and over. That chapter is about abiding in Jesus and often I would read it on my knees.

Then I started being led of the Spirit to go every day to the same place at the same hour and spend a certain amount of time praying and waiting on the Lord. As I grew spiritually, I would sometimes spend longer times there. After a while, instead of praying for a rigid, set amount of time, I would simply pray until I sensed a release in my heart and knew I was finished.

I can tell you today that if I hadn't spent those times before God during my early years, I wouldn't be doing what I am now in ministry. Some of the things the Lord spoke to me about and taught me back then are still strongly influencing my life. So you can see how important it is to follow the instructions God is giving you.

No Hollow Logs, Please

Many times instead of getting those instructions for themselves, believers who are eager to grow quickly in prayer try to get the results someone else got by duplicating their prayer life. We've all made that mistake at times.

We'll read that John Wesley prayed two hours a day and we'll say, "That's it. That's the way to be spiritual." Then we try to pray two hours a day, fail miserably and end up under condemnation.

Or maybe we'll read about revivals a hundred years ago when the people would have all-night prayer meetings. So we'll say, "Okay. Here's how we have revival. We all stay up and pray until dawn." Then we schedule a prayer meeting and by midnight half the congregation is asleep!

I even read once about a man many years ago who would pray for days in a hollow log. The squirrels would feed him. He produced powerful results in prayer. It's a good thing he's not around today. As soon as word got out, we'd be selling hollow logs in our bookstores and teaching hollow-log doctrines in our newsletters!

We need to wise up. Those people prayed for two hours, or all night, or in a hollow log because the Holy Spirit moved them to do it. He led them and He gave them the grace and the power. Even more importantly, it wasn't the number of hours they spent or the particular way they prayed that brought results. It was the fact that they yielded to the Holy Spirit. They cooperated with Him so He could bring about those results!

So stop measuring your prayer life against the prayer life of Sister Sally or Brother Ralph and start asking the Lord what He wants *you* to do about prayer.

"But He's not speaking to me about my prayer life!" you say.

Yes, He is and if you will listen, you'll find out what He is saying. I don't mean it will come blaring forth as if

He were shouting at you through a bull horn. His leadings
are usually more subtle than that. At first, you'll just sense
a little nudge in a particular direction. You'll feel drawn
toward spending a certain amount of time in prayer.
When you obey that leading, you'll find yourself with a
deep sense of satisfaction that comes from doing what
God is directing you to do.

Once you've clearly understood what God is saying
to you about your prayer life, get with the program—and
stick with it! Refuse to let anything keep you away from
your times of prayer. Get violent about it if you have to
(spiritually speaking, of course). As Matthew 11:12 KJV
says, "...the kingdom of God suffereth violence, and the
violent take it by force."

Jesus gave us a living illustration during His earthly
ministry of how fiercely protective we're to be about
prayer. You can see it in Mark 11:15-17:

> *And (Jesus and His disciples) came to
> Jerusalem. And He went into the temple
> [area, the porches and courts] and began to
> drive out those who sold and bought in the
> temple area, and He overturned the [four-
> footed] tables of the money changers and the
> seats of those who dealt in doves; and He
> would not permit anyone to carry any
> household equipment through the temple
> enclosure [thus making the temple area a
> short-cut traffic lane]. And He taught and
> said to them, Is it not written, My house
> shall be called a house of prayer for all the
> nations? But you have turned it into a den
> of robbers.*

As a powerful woman of prayer said to me once, "All
the way through your life there will be distractions that

come to lure you away from the secret place of the Most High. There will be interruptions that try to pull you away from your relationship with God. But don't give into them. Instead, take a whip of the blood of Jesus and drive those things out of your life."

Those are forceful words, aren't they? And they are well worth heeding for, in this day and hour, you and I are the House of Prayer. We must guard it well.

CHAPTER 5

Making the
Faith Connection

*And when he was come into the house, the
blind men came to him: and Jesus saith
unto them, Believe ye that I am able to do
this? They said unto him, Yea, Lord. Then
touched he their eyes, saying, According to
your faith be it unto you.* (Matthew 9:28-29)

Sometimes people who have tried to follow the leadership of the Holy Spirit and found they could discern no
clear direction from Him are afraid they will never be able to
do so. *After all,* they think, *I've been a Christian for 15
years. If I had the ability to sense the Lord's leading that
distinctly, wouldn't I have already discovered it?*

Not necessarily. One of the most remarkable charac-
ters in the Bible lived for 65 years before he made that dis-
covery. His name is Enoch and Genesis 5 says this about him:

*When Enoch was 65 years old, Methuselah
was born. Enoch walked [in habitual fellow-
ship] with God after the birth of Methuselah*

300 years and had other sons and daugh-
ters. So all the days of Enoch were 365 years.
And Enoch walked [in habitual fellowship]
with God; and he was not, for God took him
[home with Him]. (verses 21-24)

This is a very interesting situation when you think about it. For 65 years, Enoch lived a purely natural human existence. We don't know exactly what he did during that time because the Bible doesn't tell us, but we can assume he did what most people do who live average lives. He probably woke up in the morning, got dressed, ate breakfast and went to work. He came home in the evening, entertained himself for a while then went to bed.

The Bible doesn't indicate there was anything unusual about him. But suddenly, after 65 years of living the same old natural way, something changed for Enoch. We don't know exactly how it happened. Maybe he started thinking about the stories his ancestors had told him about walking with God. After all, his great- great- great- great grandfather, Adam, had known and walked with God in a very personal way.

Whatever the reason, one day it dawned on Enoch that he could live in fellowship with God. He said in his heart, *"If I reach out to God, I believe He'll reach out to me. If I talk to God, I believe He'll talk to me. If I seek Him, then I'll find Him."*

In other words, Enoch released faith and dared to believe that he could walk with God.

We know that's what happened because Hebrews 11 says:

*Because of **faith** Enoch was caught up and*
transferred to heaven, so that he did not
have a glimpse of death; and he was not
found, because God had translated him.
For even before he was taken to heaven,

*he received testimony [still on record] that he
had pleased and been satisfactory to God.
But without faith it is impossible to please
and be satisfactory to Him. For whoever
would come near to God must [necessarily]
believe that God exists and that He is the
rewarder of those who earnestly and diligently seek Him [out].* (verses 5-6)

You want to talk about someone who flowed in the
Spirit? Enoch flowed in the Spirit! He followed God so
closely that eventually he followed Him right out of this
earthly realm into the realm of heaven without ever experiencing death!

How could he do such a thing? By faith. By believing
that if he sought God diligently He would reveal Himself.

How will *you* be able to follow the leadership of the
Spirit? In exactly the same way—by faith. For as Galatians
3:5 tells us, "He Who supplies you with His marvelous [Holy]
Spirit and works powerfully and miraculously among you
(does) so...on the basis of your believing!"

Faith is what connects you to everything in the realm
of the spirit. The blessing of salvation, for example, is available to every single person on the face of the earth. Jesus has
already died and paid the price for all sin. But the only
people who can experience that blessing are those who will
dare to believe and receive it by faith. It's only accessible to
those who will say, "Yes, I believe that through the blood of
Jesus, I am forgiven of my sins and by the power of His Holy
Spirit I've been delivered from the kingdom of darkness into
the kingdom of God!"

To flow in the Spirit you must release that same kind
of faith. You must simply dare to believe God will do what
He says. If He says, "Draw nigh to God, and he will draw nigh
to you," (and He does in James 4:8 KJV) then you simply trust
Him to be true to His Word. If He says, "Call unto me, and I
will answer thee, and shew thee great and mighty things,

which thou knowest not," (and He does in Jeremiah 33:3 KJV) then you expect Him to show you things when you call on Him in prayer. Period. Without question.

If you'll look again at Hebrews 11:6, you'll see that kind of faith is what opens the door to God's manifest presence, not only in our prayer closets but in the rest of our lives as well. As the Knox-Taylor translation says, "Nobody ever reaches God's presence until he has learned to believe; believe that God exists and that He reveals Himself to those who sincerely look for Him."

God Is Not Hiding From You

If we are to follow the leadership of the Holy Spirit, we must put behind us the idea that it is difficult to talk God into revealing Himself to us. God isn't playing games with us. He isn't trying to be mysterious. He *wants to reveal Himself to us. It's His nature to do so.*

Someone might say, "Well, it seems to me He hides more than He reveals."

In one way, that's true; for Isaiah 45:15 NIV says of Him, "Truly you are a God who hides himself, O God, and Savior of Israel."

There's no denying the fact that if God so chose, He could manifest Himself so clearly there would not be one person on the face of the earth who would question His existence. He could shake this planet and reveal Himself in such power that there would be no agnostics and no atheists to be found. But He doesn't do that.

Instead, He has chosen to set up a particular criteria. He has chosen to hide Himself from those who don't meet that criteria and He has chosen to reveal Himself to those who do. Hebrews 11:6 clearly tells us what that criteria is. It is *faith.*

Of course, we all realize we need faith for our initial salvation experience. But many Christians think once they are born again such faith isn't necessary anymore. Thus, they'll see someone who knows the Lord better and hears

His voice more clearly than they do and they'll think that person is just somehow different than they are. "Well, you know, she has a special calling on her life to pray," they'll say. "That's why she's so sensitive spiritually."

No, that's not the reason. The Bible says, "God is no respecter of persons" (Acts 10:34 KJV). He doesn't just make some people more spiritual than others. He reveals Himself to those who continue to seek Him in faith. He makes Himself known to those who reach out to Him, confidently expecting Him to reward them with a deeper knowledge of Himself!

The reason some people feel that God hides Himself and stays a million miles away when they pray, is because they haven't released that kind of faith. They haven't come in childlike trust and said, "Lord, I don't care how unspiritual I may feel right now, You said in Your Word You would draw near to me if I'd draw near to You. So I'm drawing near to You right now, believing You are right here with me and I'm expecting You to reward me with Your manifest presence."

Actually, the Bible says He *is* right there with you—whether you believe it or not. But lack of faith keeps you from experiencing Him. As Acts 17:24-28 KJV says:

> *God that made the world and all things there-in, seeing that he is Lord of heaven and earth, dwelleth not in temples made with hands; nei-ther is worshipped with men's hands, as though he needed any thing, seeing he giveth to all life, and breath, and all things; And hath made of one blood all nations of men for to dwell on all the face of the earth, and hath determined the times before appointed, and the bounds of their habitation; that they should seek the Lord, if haply they might feel after him, and find him, though he be not far from every one of us: for in him we live, and move, and have our being...*

God is not far from us. He is all around us. And the more we'll release our faith and seek Him, sincerely believing that He will reveal Himself to us, the more intimately we'll know Him and experience Him.

Are You Traveling by Concorde...or Pony Express?

"I'm sure that's true, Sister Hammond. But I just don't have that kind of faith."

Then go to the Bible and get some! After all, "faith cometh by hearing, and hearing by the word of God" (Romans 10:17 KJV). Develop your faith to flow in the Holy Spirit by studying and meditating on the promises God has given us about Him.

That's what I did. When I first began praying, I knew I had no ability in myself to pray effectively. (Since almost all I could think of to say was, "Lord, help me!" it didn't take me long to figure that out.) I didn't know much of the Word of God either, but I had seen Romans 8:26-27.

> *So too the [Holy] Spirit comes to our aid and bears us up in our weakness; for we do not know what prayer to offer nor how to offer it worthily as we ought, but the Spirit Himself goes to meet our supplication and pleads in our behalf with unspeakable yearnings and groanings too deep for utterance. And He Who searches the hearts of men knows what is in the mind of the [Holy] Spirit [what His intent is], because the Spirit intercedes and pleads [before God] in behalf of the saints according to and in harmony with God's will.*

When I saw that promise, I simply believed it. I began expecting the Holy Spirit to help me pray. I had no idea how He would do it, but that wasn't my concern. I just assumed since He was God, He was smart enough to figure out how to get through to me.

My confidence grew even more when I read what Jesus had to say in John 14 through 16 about how the Holy Spirit would teach and reveal the things of God to me. Even though I was just starting out in the things of the Spirit, I was confident that as I continued to pray and trust the Spirit to teach and reveal things to me, He most certainly would.

When I look back at those days now, it amazes me how God developed me. At first, my prayers were quite simple. Whether I was praying in English or in tongues, they seemed very repetitious. But as I continued to meditate the promises of God and increase in my faith to be led by the Holy Spirit, my ability to pray increased as well. Of course, that didn't happen overnight. But gradually, the more I grew in faith, the more deeply I could reach into my heart and pull out the prayers God had put inside me.

You may think it's strange to talk about pulling prayers out of your heart, but it's actually quite scriptural. After all, the Bible says the Holy Spirit dwells within us and He has many things about which He wants to pray. His very nature is to pray. That's why the Bible calls Him the *Spirit of grace and supplication* (Zechariah 12:10). Where are those prayers He wants to pray? They're on the inside of us where He is. They're in our hearts. But we must draw them out.

That's why faith is so important right now. God is wanting the Church to bring forth great things in prayer and it requires faith for us to do that. You see, in prayer we *always* travel by faith. It is like a vehicle that takes us from where we are to where we want to go. And the size of our faith determines whether we travel by Concorde or by pony express.

Some people have tried to separate the *prayer of faith* and put it in a category all by itself. They've said, "This particular kind of prayer is the only one in which you release faith." But they're mistaken. Every kind of prayer requires faith. It doesn't matter whether you're praying the prayer of faith, prayer of agreement, worship, intercession, supplication, or any other kind of prayer, if you're not releasing faith you're not going anywhere.

You could pray all night long and heaven will hardly notice if you're not praying in faith. You could cry, quote scripture, and rebuke the Devil in the grandest way but if when you are finished you do not believe that something has happened in the realm of the spirit in response to your prayer, you have wasted your time.

Develop Your Faith to Follow the Spirit

It amazes me how many Christians who have been taught about faith in the Word of God, have so little faith in their ability to follow the leadership of the Holy Spirit. They have great faith in other areas. Ask them, for example, if God will get them to heaven when they die, and they'll answer a confident, faith-filled, "Yes!" Ask them if He'll heal them or prosper them or deliver them from trouble. "Yes!" they'll say.

But ask them if He'll speak to them and reveal exactly how they need to pray about a certain situation and they'll say, "Well, you know, I've just never been able to hear the voice of God that clearly."

Why is that? It's because they haven't developed their faith in that area.

I discovered early in my Christian life that if I wanted to develop faith for healing, I had to spend time reading and meditating on what God's Word said about healing. If I wanted to develop faith for finances, I had to spend time on scriptures about prosperity. And if I wanted to develop faith to flow in the Holy Spirit, I had to focus my attention on what God's Word said about the operation of the Holy Spirit in my life.

That's why I've spent untold hours since 1972 reading and studying what Jesus said to the disciples in John 14 through 16. I found that the more I would feed on His promises about the Spirit, the more my prayer life would develop.

Even now, after all these years, I still read about the work of the Holy Spirit almost every day because I want to be continually aware of Him. Have you ever heard the phrase *Out of sight, out of mind?* The reverse of that is also true. Whatever you keep before your eyes, whatever you focus your attention upon spiritually, will be an active force in your life.

Of course, many Christians already know what the Bible has to say about the Holy Spirit. They can quote the scriptures. They can even teach them to others. But because they haven't released faith, expecting those scriptural truths to be manifested in their lives, their knowledge hasn't helped them much.

If that's been your experience, as we examine those scriptures again through these next few pages, I urge you to take a fresh look at them. Don't just read them for information, receive them as living promises from God Himself to you. Spend time thinking about them, confessing them and acting on them in prayer. As Colossians 3:16 KJV says, "Let the word of Christ dwell in you richly," and dare to believe that what the Bible says the Holy Spirit will do— He will do *in you!*

CHAPTER 6

The Work of the Holy Spirit

For as many as are led by the Spirit of God, they are the sons of God.
(Romans 8:14 KJV)

First and most importantly, we must learn from the scriptures who the Holy Spirit actually is. Contrary to popular belief, He is not some vague, vaporous influence, difficult for the normal Christian to detect, much less follow. No, the Holy Spirit is a person and every child of God has the ability to recognize Him.

In fact, His presence and person can be as distinctly familiar to us as the presence and person of Jesus was to His disciples during His earthly ministry. God has given us the spiritual capacity to see Him so clearly with the eyes of our heart and know Him so intimately that we can follow Him just as the disciples followed Jesus.

We know that is true because Jesus said just before He went to the cross:

*[Dear] little children. I am to be with you only
a little longer. You will look for Me and, as I told
the Jews, so I tell you now: you are not able to
come where I am going...You are not able to
follow Me now where I am going, but you shall
follow Me afterwards. (John 13:33, 36)*

Think about that statement for a moment. How were
the disciples to follow Jesus after His death and resurrection when He was no longer on the earth? They wouldn't
be able to see His physical body. They wouldn't be able to
hear His voice with their physical ears. So how were they
to do it?

The same way we follow Him today—through the
leadership of the Holy Spirit. Jesus explained that to them
just a few verses later when He said:

*And I will ask the Father, and He will give you
another Comforter (Counselor, Helper, Intercessor,
Advocate, Strengthener, and Standby), that He
may remain with you forever—the Spirit of
Truth, Whom the world cannot receive (welcome,
take to its heart), because it does not see Him or
know and recognize Him. But you know and recognize Him, for He lives with you [constantly]
and will be in you. (John 14:16-17)*

Do you see what that last sentence says? It says *you
will know and recognize Him*. It doesn't say you might
recognize Him if you're a super-spiritual person. It doesn't
say a few gifted people will know Him. It simply says you
will know Him. Therefore, if you've had doubts about your
ability to recognize the Holy Spirit, you can put those
doubts out of your mind. Jesus Himself has given you His
Word that you can do it.

Of course, getting to know the Holy Spirit is just like
getting to know anyone else—it takes time. But the moment

you release your faith and believe you have the capacity to know Him, the process will begin.

Some people say, "Oh, I just wish I had known Jesus like the disciples knew Him. I'd be able to follow Him much more closely if I'd just been with Him in the flesh like they were."

Those people have missed the magnificence of the relationship with Jesus that is available to us today. They don't realize we can get to know Him much better through the Holy Spirit than the disciples knew Him during His earthly ministry.

You see, Jesus had natural limitations because He lived in a flesh-and-blood body. He couldn't be speaking with every disciple every moment of the day. He couldn't respond to their every thought and direct their every step. That would have been physically impossible for Him.

But now, through the precious person of the Holy Spirit, He can do all those things. He can be there the moment we open our eyes in the morning, speaking to us. He can guide us personally every hour of the day. Every time we sit down to read the Bible, He is there causing the Word to come alive within us, illumining our hearts and revealing God's will.

Just think, the Holy Spirit can fellowship with us 24 hours a day, every day of our lives! He can help us with every single decision—great or small. He can be there constantly to comfort us, counsel us, help us, intercede for us, strengthen us and stand by us.

No wonder Jesus said:

> *I am telling you nothing but the truth when*
> *I say it is profitable (good, expedient, advan-*
> *tageous) for you that I go away. Because if I*
> *do not go away, the Comforter (Counselor,*
> *Helper, Advocate, Intercessor, Strengthener,*
> *Standby) will not come to you [into close*
> *fellowship with you]; but if I go away, I will*
> *send Him to you...*(John 16:7)

The Holy Spirit Reveals Jesus

"Wait a minute!" you may say. "I'm confused. Exactly who am I supposed to follow—Jesus or the Holy Spirit?"

Actually, the answer is *both*. For as the Holy Spirit fellowships with us, He reveals Jesus to us. He shows us what Jesus wants us to see. He speaks to us the words Jesus wants us to hear. That's His job and if we'll simply allow Him to do it by releasing our faith, He will make Jesus more near to us and dear to us than anyone else could ever be. He'll help us see Jesus so clearly that following Him becomes very easy.

It's a simple matter to follow someone when you can see them, isn't it? You don't have to sit around and wonder about it. You don't have to work very hard to figure out how to do it. You just watch them and then go where they go.

That's the kind of simplicity Jesus intended for us to enjoy through our relationship with the Holy Spirit. That's why He said:

> *I will not leave you as orphans [comfortless, desolate, bereaved, forlorn, helpless]; I will come [back] to you. Just a little while now, and the world will not see Me any more, but you will see Me; because I live, you will live also. At that time [when that day comes] you will know [for yourselves] that I am in My Father, and you [are] in Me, and I [am] in you. The person who has My commands and keeps them is the one who [really] loves Me; and whoever [really] loves Me will be loved by My Father, and I [too] will love him and will show (reveal, manifest) Myself to him. [I will let Myself be clearly seen by him and make Myself real to him.]* (John 14:18-21)

"But if seeing and following Jesus is so simple," you ask, "why is it such a struggle for most of us?"

As I said before, it is because we haven't cultivated our faith in this area. We haven't believed and expected the

Holy Spirit to do for us everything Jesus said He would do. Therefore we haven't developed this wonderful resource God has given us.

Jesus Himself said in John 14:29 that He told us these things about the Holy Spirit so we would *believe* them. Why is it so important that we believe them? Because the Bible says it will be unto you *according to your faith* (Matthew 9:29). If by faith you expect the Holy Spirit to reveal Jesus to you and make Him clear to you, then He'll be able to do that. If you sit around in unbelief and say, "I just can't hear God's voice like other people do," you'll cut short the Holy Spirit's work in you.

Understanding How the Spirit Leads

Believe me, God is big enough to speak to you. I don't care how dense you think you are, God knows exactly how to get His communications through to your heart. He didn't have any trouble speaking to a donkey in the Old Testament (Numbers 22) so He can surely handle you!

Exactly how will He speak? In many different ways. One thing the Bible says He'll do, for example, is bring the Word of God to your remembrance. If you've been a believer for very long, you've probably already experienced that part of His ministry. Maybe you were going through a tough situation or facing a difficult decision when suddenly a particular scripture came to mind and gave you just the insight you needed at the time.

Whether you realized it or not—that was the Holy Spirit speaking to you! Jesus promised us He would do that in John 14:26 KJV. There He said, "...the Comforter, which is the Holy Ghost, whom the Father will send in my name, he shall teach you all things, and bring all things to your remembrance, whatsoever I have said unto you."

In John 16:13, Jesus reveals some other very important things we can expect the Holy Spirit to do for us.

...When He, the Spirit of Truth (the Truth-giving Spirit) comes, He will guide you into all the Truth (the whole, full Truth). For He will not speak His own message [on His own authority]; but He will tell whatever He hears [from the Father; He will give the message that has been given to Him], and He will announce and declare to you the things that are to come [that will happen in the future]. (John 16:13)

God never intended for Christians to watch the news on television and then go pray about what they saw. He sent the Holy Spirit to show us things to come so we could pray about those things in advance. If we'd just learn to tune into the Spirit, we would know what's happening long before the news stations do!

When I first realized that, I was thrilled. I didn't know how God was going to deliver the information to me, but I took Him at His Word anyway. I said, "Lord, You said right here the Holy Spirit would show me things to come. So I'm just expecting You to do that for me and I'm thanking You for it right now!"

Sure enough, He did. I remember one time during those early years when I first began to make prayer my priority, I had a sense there was something specific God wanted me to lift up to Him in prayer. I didn't really know what it was, I could just feel something stirring in my heart. So I went to my prayer room and just began praying in tongues, waiting on the Lord and seeking His direction.

After a few minutes, the Holy Spirit began leading me very strongly to pray for things hidden to be revealed. As I prayed along those lines, I realized I was praying about the government. It seemed to me as I prayed, I was pulling out things that had been kept secret, exposing wrongs that had been covered up. Some months later, the break-in at Watergate was revealed to the public. No doubt the reporters who uncovered the story thought they were the first to find out about it, but they weren't. The Holy Spirit had been leading people to pray about it long before the newspapers printed their first line!

Please understand, however, when I say the Holy Spirit led me in a direction or spoke something to my heart, I don't mean He dealt with me in a dramatic way. It wasn't as though dynamite went off inside me or a shaft of light shined down from heaven. The Holy Spirit is normally much more quiet and subtle than that.

His leadings sometimes come as the gentle reminders we read about in John 14:26. At other times, they take the forms described in John 16:14-15. There Jesus says:

> *...[the Holy Spirit] will honor and glorify Me,*
> *because He will take of (receive, draw upon)*
> *what is Mine and will reveal (declare,*
> *disclose, transmit) it to you. Everything*
> *that the Father has is Mine. That is what I*
> *meant when I said that He [the Spirit] will*
> *take the things that are Mine and will reveal*
> *(declare, disclose, transmit) it to you.*

I love the words the Amplified Bible uses there to describe the communications of the Holy Spirit because they so accurately capture what He does for us.

Sometimes He *declares* things to us. He speaks to our hearts so clearly and definitely, it's almost as though we can hear it with our natural ears. At other times, He *discloses* or *reveals* things to us. We might just be praying along fellowshipping with the Lord when suddenly we'll glimpse a new truth. An image will flash in our spirit and it will forever change our perspective. It will allow us to exchange our own, limited human viewpoint for the eternal viewpoint of God.

I remember reading about a great, praying man named George Mueller who lived during the 1800's. It is said that he prayed for the salvation of one particular fellow for many years with no apparent results. Yet he was absolutely confident that the man would ultimately be saved.

What was the source of that confidence? In times of prayer, he had seen that fellow rejoicing in heaven before God's throne. The Holy Spirit had disclosed or revealed that image to his heart. As it turned out, the man was saved after the death of that dear, praying saint.

Not only will the Holy Spirit declare and disclose, at times He will also *transmit* things to you. When that happens to me, it's as though He slips me a thought without my even realizing it. I just might be cleaning my house or brushing my teeth when this wonderful truth will float up from my heart. I used to wonder where such thoughts came from. But now I know—they come from the Holy Spirit!

The Bible also says the Holy Spirit will *teach* us. What will He teach us? Anything we need to know! 1 John 2:27 puts it this way:

> *But as for you, the anointing (the sacred appointment, the unction) which you received from Him abides [permanently] in you; [so] then you have no need that anyone should instruct you. But just as His anointing teaches you concerning everything and is true and is no falsehood, so you must abide in (live in, never depart from) Him [being rooted in Him, knit to Him], just as [His anointing] has taught you [to do].*

When God's Desires Become Your Own

If you'll read the last phrase in that passage again, you'll notice it specifically mentions one particular thing the Holy Spirit (or the anointing) will teach you to do and that is to abide in Him. What does it mean to abide somewhere? It means to live there, to dwell there on a continual basis.

You see, God never meant for us to just tune into the Holy Spirit now and then. He didn't plan for us to fellowship with Him only when we're in our prayer closet. God intended for us to abide continually in the presence of His Spirit. He meant for us to converse with Him all day long.

Do you know you can train your heart to be constantly aware of the companionship of the Holy Spirit? Do you know you can develop yourself spiritually to the point where you interact with Him not just when you read the Bible or pray or go to church, but when you're eating breakfast, getting dressed, driving to work, cooking dinner, or doing anything else?

You absolutely can! And you don't have to be some sort of weird, super-saint to do it, either. In fact, Jesus commanded us all to live that way. As far as He is concerned that is just basic Christianity. He said:

> *Dwell in Me, and I will dwell in you. [Live in Me, and I will live in you.] Just as no branch can bear fruit of itself without abiding in (being vitally united to) the vine, neither can you bear fruit unless you abide in Me. I am the Vine; you are the branches. Whoever lives in Me and I in him bears much (abundant) fruit. However, apart from Me [cut off from vital union with Me] you can do nothing. If a person does not dwell in Me, he is thrown out like a [broken-off] branch, and withers; such branches are gathered up and thrown into the fire, and they are burned. If you live in Me [abide vitally united to Me] and My words remain in you and continue to live in your hearts, ask whatever you will, and it shall be done for you. (John 15:4-7)*

Ask whatever you will, and it shall be done for you! That's a wonderful prayer promise, isn't it? But never forget it is made to the person who abides in Jesus and in His Word. And we can only abide through constant fellowship with the Holy Spirit.

As I mentioned earlier, the word *ask* used there has a deeper significance than most people realize. Its Greek meaning implies your will and God's will are so closely intertwined, when you ask for something, it is because He is asking for it as well. That's what happens to praying people who continually fellowship with the Holy Spirit. He begins to put God's desires in their heart so that when they pray, they're not making silly, superficial requests based on their own selfish whims, they're lifting up God's own desires.

They're praying His perfect will. Yet, they are praying their own will as well because His will has become their will.

That's not really surprising. You can see the same thing happen in natural, human friendships. Say, for example, you have a dear friend whose son has run away from home. Day after day you fellowship with your friend about the situation. You weep with him about it. You share his sorrow.

Before long, your desire for his child to come home grows almost as strong as your friend's desire. Your love for him and your fellowship with him has caused his need to become your need, his yearning to become your own.

That's exactly what happens as you fellowship with the Holy Spirit. He confides in you the longings of the Father's heart. He causes God's own dreams to stir so strongly within you that eventually you find His divine requests flowing from your own lips. And when that happens, you can surely ask whatever you will and it will be done.

CHAPTER 7

Daily Time in the Word

*M*an shall not live by bread alone, but by
every word that proceedeth out of the mouth
of God. (Matthew 4:4 KJV)

Jesus said each one of us is a house of prayer and in
every orderly house, there are rules of conduct that set the
tone there. There are certain habits—say, taking out the
trash or buying groceries—that help the household to run
smoothly.

The same is true in your house of prayer. Even though
prayer itself is a matter of the heart, there are a few prayer
habits you can adopt that will benefit you greatly in your personal prayer life.

The first and most vital is the simple habit of spending
time reading and meditating on the Word of God—not just
once in a while, but every single day. God's Word is essential
to your prayer life. It is the fuel behind every effective
prayer. When your Word level gets low, you'll find your
prayers sputtering and lurching along instead of roaring
ahead in power. If you don't stop and refuel, your praying
will eventually come to a complete stop.

Hebrews 1:3 tells us that God Himself is "upholding and maintaining and guiding and propelling the universe by His mighty word of power." If God's Word is the force behind the entire universe, obviously it must be the force behind our prayers as well.

Jesus left no room for doubt about that. For in the gospel of John, He forever linked the Word with answered prayer by saying, "If ye abide in me, **and my words abide in you**, ye shall ask what ye will, and it shall be done unto you" (John 15:7 KJV).

A Daily Feast

Some people have tried to take a spiritual shortcut by simply pulling scriptures out of the Bible and inserting them in their prayers, thinking that just because they've used scriptural words, their prayers will take on supernatural power. But there's more to praying the Word than parroting biblical phrases. For the Word to truly give power to our prayers, it must take up residence in our heart. We must meditate upon it until it becomes revelation from the Holy Spirit and dwells richly within us (Colossians 3:16).

Once that happens, the Word of God is no longer just a bunch of ideas in a leather-bound book. It is "alive and full of power...active, operative, energizing, and effective" (Hebrews 4:12). It literally brings life to us.

People everywhere are looking for life. But most of them are looking in the wrong places. Some folks think exercise will give them life, so they spend all their time at the health club. Others seem to think vitamins will give them life, so they spend all their time at the health food store. Still others have the idea that relaxing will give them life, so they spend every possible moment on vacation.

But the reality is, even though each of those things is fine, the only place you can actually go to get life is the Word of God. That's because the Word contains the very substance of God Himself. It's not just nice-sounding phrases. It is real spiritual substance.

When you get your Bible and begin to read and meditate on the Word, the Holy Spirit imparts that substance to you. You partake of the very life and nature of God Himself. (See 2 Peter 1:4.) I'm not talking just about a mental effect or a little spiritual influence. I'm saying that as you receive God's Word, His power is transmitted to you.

You see, the Words of God "are spirit, and they are life" (John 6:63). They do for your inner man what food does for your outer man. Just as the food you eat supplies energy to your physical body, when you digest the Word of God it supplies you with spiritual energy. That's why the apostle Paul admonished Timothy to be "a good minister of Jesus Christ, nourished up in the words of faith" (1 Timothy 4:6). God's Word is spiritual nourishment.

Over the years, I've noticed people who feed their spirit constantly with the Word of God can more easily follow their hearts. I believe that's because the heart has grown so strong, it exerts a greater pull on them than their flesh does. The reverse is also true. People who don't feed on the Word have a more difficult time following their heart because it is weak. And often, the strong voice of their well-fed flesh drowns out the faint cry of their frail spirit.

Remember this: you cannot be weak in spirit and strong in prayer. That is a complete impossibility, for real prayer requires you to become a co-laborer with God. It requires you to grasp His will and His plan about a particular matter and lift it up to heaven with the fervency and heat that comes from the very heart of God Himself.

Do you think a spiritual weakling could accomplish so great a task? Certainly not! The Bible says we must be *strong to apprehend and grasp* the love of God (Ephesians 3:18-19) and no one ever grew strong in God without feeding upon His Word.

Notice I said you grow strong by *feeding* on the Word *(present tense)*, not by *having been fed* on it *(past tense)*. You'll never get anywhere spiritually by going to church once in a while and reading your Bible only on occasion. You need a constant supply of the Word. For it's the Word that is fresh and alive in you today, it's the truth that is proceeding from the mouth of God into your heart right now that will work most powerfully in you.

The Old Testament tells us that when God sent manna to feed the children of Israel in the wilderness, they had to gather it every day except the Sabbath. If they tried to store it, it would spoil. The Word of God is much the same way. So we must feed on it not just once or twice a week—but every single day!

Keys to Meditation

Although the Bible says a great deal about meditating on the Word, many Christians don't really know how to do it. As a result, they end up reading chapter after chapter of their Bible without benefiting from it as they should.

If that has been the case with you, let me encourage you to concentrate more on the quality of your time in the Word. Instead of trying to digest five or six chapters all at once, pick out one shorter passage of scripture that especially speaks to your heart. If you're going through a time when you particularly need God's protection, for example, you could select Psalm 91:2 KJV. "I will say of the Lord, He is my *refuge* and my fortress: my God; in him will I trust." Then you could deepen your understanding of it by cross referencing the word refuge in your concordance and read every scriptural reference to it throughout the Bible.

You can also meditate on the Word by vividly imagining individual Bible stories. If you're needing healing, you might pick the story in Mark 10 about the blind beggar, Bartimaeus. That is one of my personal favorites because at a time in my life when I was desperately ill, I read that story hundreds of times.

Actually, I didn't just read it—I lived it. I would picture Jericho in my mind. I'd see Jesus walking with His disciples and the crowds gathered all around. I'd imagine how Bartimaeus felt as he frantically cried out to get Jesus' attention, and I'd hear the voices of the people around him as they scolded him saying, "Be quiet, Bartimaeus! Who do you think you are? Keep your mouth shut!"

Then in my mind's eye, I'd see myself in Bartimaeus' place. I would see Jesus calling me to Him. Then I'd see myself jumping up and throwing off my illness just like Bartimaeus threw off the cloak that signified his blindness. I would see myself healed!

Using your imagination this way is an extremely powerful method of transferring the scriptures from your head to your heart. It will make the Bible come alive for you as never before.

The third way you can meditate on the Word is to take a verse of scripture and carry it with you all day long. I don't mean you should put a Bible in your purse or your pocket and carry it with you. I mean, put a scripture in your mind and heart and just think about it night and day, turning it over and over in your mind.

You must understand, however, for the power of the Word to be fully activated in your life, you must believe it and act on it. James 1:22-25 puts it this way:

> *But be doers of the Word [obeying the mes-*
> *sage], and not merely listeners to it, betray-*
> *ing yourselves [into deception...]. For if*
> *anyone only listens to the Word without*
> *obeying it and being a doer of it, he is like*
> *a man who looks carefully at his [own]*
> *natural face in a mirror; for he thoughtfully*
> *observes himself, and then goes off and*
> *promptly forgets what he was like. But he*
> *who looks carefully into the faultless law of*
> *liberty, and is faithful to it and perseveres in*
> *looking into it, being not a heedless listener*
> *who forgets but an active doer [who obeys],*
> *he shall be blessed in his doing.*

I Know That Voice!

If you'll make daily meditation and obedience to the Word a habit, it will protect you from getting drawn into the errors that sometimes crop up among people who pray. That's because God's Word is truth (John 17:17) and truth always dispels error.

As you meditate on the Word, you're actually fellowshipping with the Spirit of Truth. You're growing familiar with His voice. Have you ever known someone so well that when they call you on the phone, they don't even have to identify themselves? They just say, "Hello!" and instantly you know who they are.

That's what happens as you listen to the Holy Spirit speak to you through the words of the Bible. You get to know Him so well you can recognize His voice anywhere. He might speak to you in the grocery store and your spirit will jump up and say, "I know that voice! That's the One who speaks to me through the scriptures every day."

By the same token, when the Devil tries to trick you with some foolish and unscriptural doctrine, he won't be able to fool you. The moment you hear it, your heart will draw back. "Wait a minute," you'll say. "That's not the Holy Spirit. That's the voice of a stranger and I will not follow it!"

Assured of the Answer

Perhaps the greatest blessing of spending daily time in God's Word is the sense of assurance it gives us when we pray. For the more firmly our prayers are grounded in God's Word, the more sure we can be that those prayers will be answered. As 1 John 5:14-15 KJV says:

> *This is the confidence that we have in him, that, if we ask any thing according to his will, he heareth us: and if we know that he hear us, whatsoever we ask, we know that we have the petitions that we desired of him.*

When our prayers are fueled by the Word and filled with the faith only it can generate, we can be absolutely certain we are praying according to God's will. We do not have to waver in our faith, wondering if He will give us what we ask. We can simply rejoice, knowing without a doubt our answer is on the way!

CHAPTER 8

Keeping a Prayer Notebook

Write the vision, and make it plain upon
tables, that he may run that readeth it.
(Habakkuk 2:2 KJV)

Another habit I have found to be of great value in my prayer life is that of keeping a notebook with me when I pray. I use it not to makes notes in advance on what I plan to pray about (I've already told you how poorly I do with prayer lists) but to note afterward how the Spirit led and what He said to me as I prayed.

There are several reasons why this is helpful. First of all, taking a notebook puts you in an attitude of expectancy. The very fact that you have it beside you as you pray indicates you are expecting God to speak to you. That is exactly as it should be. After all, prayer is not supposed to be a monologue. It is a dialogue, a conversation between you and God.

Since God responds to your faith, when you go to

prayer expecting Him to speak to you He will most certainly accomodate you. And, needless to say, your times of prayer will be much more satisfying.

Knowing you will have to write down the things you prayed about will also encourage you to find a focus for your prayers. You'll be less likely to meander here and there without any direction. Because you'll want something specific to put in your notebook, you'll be more inclined to press in and get guidance from the Holy Spirit for your time of prayer.

Discovering Your Prayer Patterns

Another great advantage of keeping a prayer notebook is that it helps you identify the particular way in which God works with you. As you note the things He leads you to pray about, day after day, you'll begin to notice certain patterns. You'll find some issues tend to remain more strongly on your heart than others.

Over the years, I've noticed that some people continually have a burden, or a strong leading, to pray for the government. Some are drawn to pray for the body of Christ. Others are consistently led to pray for the nation of Israel, or another nation, or issue. At our church we set up prayer groups so people with such burdens can pray together. Since they have similar Holy Ghost assignments in prayer, they generally flow together better than people who have different assignments. What's more, once they learn to go with that flow they are able to bring forth much greater things corporately than they could individually.

It has been a great encouragement to me, personally, to learn how God uses me in prayer. One thing I've discovered, for instance, is I usually pray about things approximately two years in advance. Actually, I didn't notice that pattern on my own. A minister that I've prayed for, for many years brought it to my attention. He said when I would tell him the things I was praying for his ministry, he'd think I was off track. But then, those things would come to pass two years later.

Since I keep a journal, I was able to check on his observations. Sure enough, in some instances the length of time between my prayer and the manifestation was approximately two years.

Your Notebook Will Help You Remember

Not only do those kinds of records help you discover prayer patterns, they also give you confidence in your ability to hear from God. They confirm to you that the Holy Spirit truly is leading you when you pray. If you don't keep a notebook, however, you're likely to forget the details of your prayers by the time those prayers are answered.

I know it's true because I've done it. On September 11, 1988, I prayed with a group at our church about a war in the desert. We prayed about that war for six days straight. Quite often during our prayer meetings, we'll have one person sit out and take notes and because we did, we had detailed records of the things we prayed.

We prayed about warriors and land mines. We prayed about the tyrant who must be stopped and the young men who needed the moonlight to light their way through the hard terrain. Here are just a few quotes from the notes we kept during those prayer meetings:

> *There is a way, Lord. You know the way.*
> *Strengthen the leaders and show them. The*
> *North, they're coming from the North. Allies*
> *working together. We clear the airways. Lord,*
> *You send the angels, legions of angels to take*
> *them across there. Code Cobra! The invasion,*
> *a mammoth invasion. A sovereign move of*
> *God not lasting more than two months.*

You wouldn't think I would forget such prayer meetings, would you? But I did because, at the time, I didn't understand what we were praying. That's how it is sometimes when you're praying by the unction of the Holy Spirit. The things you pray seem so strange, you would never tell anyone you prayed them!

A couple of years later, however, after the war with Iraq, a friend of mine reminded me about those meetings. Even then, I had only a vague recollection so I dug through the prayer notebooks and found the notes.

I want you to know, it set our hearts afire when we read them and realized just how accurately the Holy Spirit had led us to pray for that war. He had even given us the military name for the ground troop invasion—Code Cobra. What a wonderful confirmation of the Holy Spirit's ability to speak to us and our ability to hear Him! Yet, we would have missed out on the richness of that blessing if we hadn't kept a notebook.

CHAPTER 9

Good Things Come to Those Who Wait

Wait on the Lord: be of good courage, and he shall strengthen thine heart: wait, I say, on the Lord. (Psalm 27:14 KJV)

In addition to establishing habits, you can also cultivate attitudes that will greatly enhance the atmosphere in your house of prayer. One of the most important is the attitude of dependence on the Lord.

Whether we realize it or not, we *are* totally dependent upon Him—especially in the area of prayer. The Bible tells us very plainly "we do not know what prayer to offer nor how to offer it worthily as we ought" (Romans 8:26). Therefore, if we're ever to pray effectively we must first come to a place of humility and childlike dependence. We must be able to say in all sincerity, "Father, I cannot accomplish anything without the leadership of Your Spirit. So I'm waiting here before You in reverence and faith, trusting You to show me the way I need to pray today."

Then we must be willing to do exactly what we said we would do—wait.

That may sound simple, but once you've tried it you'll find it is anything *but* simple. In this day and age, we're not used to waiting. We live in a fast-paced automated world where you put your quarter in the machine, hit the button and—*wham!*—your soft drink falls out. You put a box in the microwave, wait a few seconds and—*beep!*—dinner is served.

God, however, is not a machine. He is not a microwave. It takes time for us to cultivate a relationship with Him, not just time spent talking, either, but time spent in quiet waiting.

The fact is, most of us do too much talking in our prayer times. We need to change that. We need to stop focusing so much on what we want to say to God and start attending instead to what He wants to say to us. We need to ask for grace to cultivate the listening side of prayer.

It takes great grace, great discipline and great desire, to come to a place where we can consistently hear God's voice. It is the highest challenge of the Christian life. But we must meet that challenge, for it is the key that opens every door. Why is it so hard for us to listen? Because it often takes time for us to hear from Him. It takes the ability to wait in His presence, to quiet our minds and our hearts so the static and noise that often keep us deaf to His gentle voice melt away and we can hear Him at last.

The problem is most of us can't seem to sit still that long. We have too many other things we could (and think we should) be doing. Imagine for a moment that I were to put you in a rowboat on the middle of the ocean. If I left you there alone without an oar and told you to wait for me until I came back for you, it would be easy for you to wait, wouldn't it? There would be nothing else for you to do.

If I were to take you downtown, however, drop you off at a major intersection and tell you to wait for me, you might find waiting much more difficult—especially if I delayed in coming for you. Rather than sit helplessly on the corner, you'd have a great number of options. You could hail a cab or catch a bus. You could step into a phone booth and call a friend. You'd probably do it, too, because we all find it much more comfortable to take action and take control than to wait.

Yet, if we are to cultivate a living, vibrant relationship with God, we must learn to wait.

I've noticed in prayer groups, people who haven't developed the skill of waiting on the Lord sometimes miss God's direction because they feel they have to do something the moment prayer begins. Like a cat jumping on a mouse, they pounce on the first thing that comes into their mind and off they go, praying as fast and as hard as they can. They don't understand that sometimes God doesn't want us to *do,* He just wants us to *be.*

There are times He just wants us to get comfortable in His presence. Times when He simply wants us to set our hearts on Him and be aware both of our desperate need for Him and of His promise to fill that need to overflowing. Wonderful things happen during those quiet times. God moves on our hearts. We may not even know what He is doing, but if our hearts are turned toward Him in faith we can be sure He is doing something great.

He Works While You Wait

Even though waiting may seem like a very passive activity to you, it actually sets God in motion. Isaiah 64:4 says, "For from of old no one has heard nor perceived by the ear, nor has the eye seen a God besides You, Who works and shows Himself active on behalf of him who [earnestly] waits for Him."

Exactly what kind of work does He do for us while we wait? He strengthens us, for one thing.

Have you not known? Have you not heard?
The everlasting God, the Lord, the Creator of

*the ends of the earth, does not faint or grow
weary; there is no searching of His understanding. He gives power to the faint and
weary, and to him who has no might He
increases strength [causing it to multiply
and making it to abound]. Even youths shall
faint and be weary, and [selected] young
men shall feebly stumble and fall exhausted.
But those who wait for the Lord [who expect,
look for, and hope in Him] shall change and
renew their strength and power; they shall
lift their wings and mount up [close to God]
as eagles [mount up to the sun]; they shall
run and not be weary, they shall walk and
not faint or become tired.* (Isaiah 40:28-31)

What a blessing it is to exchange our limited, human strength for the unlimited strength of God Himself! Yet many times we pass up that blessing because we don't take the time to wait. So, instead of burning brighter day by day, eventually we burn out.

A minister's wife once said to me, "You know, I am so busy in ministry I don't have time to wait before the Lord." Of course, she meant well. She loved God. But she had fallen right into the Devil's trap. He knew if she spent all her time serving people and none in the presence of God, she'd eventually dry up, run out of power and be no help to anyone.

Don't misunderstand. I'm not saying we shouldn't serve people. What I am saying is that service should come from the overflow of our relationship with God. We should be meeting people's needs not from our own puny, human resources, but from the rivers of living water that are released within our hearts during our times of quiet fellowship with Him.

No doubt, sometimes you'll want to wring your hands when you look at your schedule. You'll think, *How am I going to get all my work done if I take time out to wait on God?* The fact is, you can't in your own strength. You will have to depend on God and you express your dependence by waiting on Him. You come before Him and say, "Lord, You are my life. You are my strength. You are my ever-present help. So I'm putting everything—schedule and all—in Your Hands. I am waiting on You."

Please understand, waiting on the Lord doesn't necessarily require hours of your time, and it doesn't always have to be done just in your prayer closet. If you'll ask the Lord to help you, you can learn to wait on Him at the office during a break time, when you're driving your car, at a restaurant while you're waiting for your food—anywhere!

I remember one particular Sunday, I had planned to spend the afternoon fellowshipping with the Lord and preparing to preach the evening service. My plans were interrupted, however, when my daughter told me she needed me to take her to the mall to buy something she needed for school on Monday. Since I had purposed in my heart not to let my ministry interfere with meeting my children's needs, I set my plans aside and off we went.

As I walked through the mall with her I thought, *Lord, it looks like I won't get to spend much time alone with You before I preach tonight, so You'll just have to help me.*

Suddenly the Lord spoke to my heart. *See that seat over there?* He said. *You just sit down there, wait on Me and let your daughter go on and shop with her friend.*

That's exactly what I did. I sat down, closed my eyes and in a flash I left that mall and stepped into the presence of God. I don't know what the shoppers who passed by me thought I was doing. I probably looked like I was asleep. But I wasn't. I was having a wonderful time fellowshipping with the Lord, listening to Him and receiving the strength I needed to minister that night.

If you'll ask the Holy Spirit for His help, He'll show you many such opportunities. He'll even help you wait on Him in the midst of seemingly impossible circumstances.

I heard about one woman, for instance, who had eight children. As you can imagine, with such a large family it's practically impossible to ever get time alone. So God gave her grace and while she was stirring the oatmeal in the morning with her children all around her, she'd throw her apron over her head and say, "Well, I'll see you all later. I'm going to spend some time with God!"

If you'll seize those small opportunities, you'll be amazed what an impact it will have on your life. You can eventually train yourself into such a habit of fellowship that whenever your mind is not engaged in something particular it will return to God like a bird returns to its nest.

Granted, it's not easy to develop yourself to that point, but if you'll be diligent and trust God to give you the grace to do it, you'll eventually be able to get there. And my, what a blessing it will be when you do!

For one thing, you'll never have trouble with backsliding. You won't do things you shouldn't because you'll be constantly aware the Holy Spirit is right there with you and you won't want to offend Him.

As you cultivate a continual consciousness of God, you'll also develop a wonderful peace. You'll find you can be undisturbed even when the circumstances and people around you are in turmoil. You'll discover for yourself the truth of Isaiah 26:3 KJV. "Thou wilt keep him in perfect peace, whose mind is stayed on thee."

When you first begin to develop the skill of waiting on the Lord, I'd advise you not to try to do it for long periods of time. Start small. Initially, you might just want to wait for five minutes or so. Once you're comfortable with that, you can gradually increase the amount of time until you reach the point where you can wait on the Lord anywhere, for any length of time you desire.

Overcoming the Obstacles

I'll warn you in advance, there are a few problems we all face when we decide to wait on the Lord. The one that stops most people is the absence of God's manifest presence. All of us know God is omnipresent. We understand He is literally present with us all the time. But even so, when we cannot sense His presence, it's difficult for us to fellowship with Him.

Of course, God doesn't want us to be controlled by emotions or spiritual goosebumps, but I believe it is His will for us to experience Him. After all, His very name, *Emmanuel*, means *God with Us;* and when a person is with us, we can sense their presence.

What's more, Hebrews 10:19-22 KJV says:

> *Having therefore, brethren, boldness to enter into the holiest by the blood of Jesus, by a new and living way, which he hath consecrated for us, through the vail, that is to say, his flesh; and having an high priest over the house of God; let us draw near with a true heart in full assurance of faith...*

According to that scripture, we're not to stand around timidly wishing we could experience God. We're to go boldly into the Holy of Holies where He manifests Himself confidently believing that Jesus has made the way for us through His blood. We're to joyfully obey the instruction in Psalm 100:2 and "come before his presence."

I'll be candid with you; I don't like to wait before God in a vacuum. I want to sense His presence attending me. So when I don't, I just say, "Lord, I know You are here because Your Word says You're here. So I'm just expecting You to reveal Yourself to me."

Almost every time, He responds by helping me experience the sweet manifestation of His presence. Why is that? Is it because I'm some super person especially called to prayer? No, it's not. It's because God honors faith. And anyone who will dare to believe that God will be true to His

Word and allow them to sense Him there with them, can enjoy the wonderful sense of His presence.

The second challenge you may encounter when you begin to wait on the Lord is a wandering mind. One moment you'll be sitting quietly with your attention on the Lord and the next moment you'll find yourself wondering if you took the clothes out of the dryer, or thinking about all the things you have to do that day. Don't be discouraged when that happens. Just continue to turn your mind back toward the Lord each time it strays.

In many ways, our minds are like undisciplined children. For the most part, we haven't trained them to be obedient to the direction of our spirit. We've just let them roam around thinking whatever they want. Like toddlers who haven't yet learned to behave, they'll climb on the furniture, swing from the drapes and do anything else that occurs to them unless someone takes them firmly by the hand and says, "No, you're not going to do that. You are going to do *this!*"

In training my mind to wait on the Lord, I've found it helpful to pick a particular scripture and center my thoughts on it. The more I focus on that scripture, the easier it is to clear other thoughts from my mind and open myself to hear from the Lord. I also keep my notebook with me during those times to keep myself in an attitude of expectancy.

I've found it's important, too, to find a physically comfortable position. I usually don't try to wait on my knees because before long they start hurting. The discomfort draws my attention away from God and onto my body. On the other hand, I don't allow myself to get too cozy because I've found it's easy to lie down intending to wait on the Lord for 30 minutes...and wake up 30 minutes later.

The third problem you're likely to face in waiting on the Lord is that of distractions. The phone won't ring all morning long, but the moment you start to get quiet before God it will seem like everyone in town has decided to call you. Your neighbor will drop by for coffee. The dog will start barking.

You may feel like giving it up and saying, "This is impossible!" But don't. The Bible tells us that both Noah and Enoch walked and fellowshipped with God. They lived in days of monumental corruption and distraction. So, if they could find ways to get quiet before God and hear His voice, the Holy Spirit can help us do it too!

Wait—and Win!

As you continue to develop your skill in waiting on the Lord at different times throughout the day, you'll find yourself much more able to wait on Him about specific issues during your prayer time. If you're facing a particular decision in your life, for example, and you don't know clearly what the Lord would have you do, you can simply set the issue before God and wait for His answer.

Second Kings 19 tells us that's what Judah's King Hezekiah did. He was facing a potentially disastrous situation. The king of Assyria had sent a letter to the inhabitants of Jerusalem informing them of his intent to invade and conquer their land. The letter warned the Israelites not to believe their God could deliver them and to save themselves by simply surrendering into their enemy's hand.

Militarily, Judah did not have the might to resist the Assyrian army. Uncertain about what to do, King Hezekiah took the letter, "went up into the house of the Lord, and spread it before the Lord" (2 Kings 19:14 KJV). Then he prayed for help and waited for a word from God.

Sure enough, he received one. The prophet Isaiah sent a message telling him his prayer had been heard and said:

> *Therefore thus saith the Lord concerning the*
> *king of Assyria, He shall not come into this*
> *city, nor shoot an arrow there, nor come*
> *before it with shield, nor cast a bank against*

it. By the way that he came, by the same
shall he return, and shall not come into this
city, saith the Lord. For I will defend this city,
to save it, for mine own sake, and for my
servant David's sake. (2 Kings 19:32-34 KJV)

In short God said, "Don't worry about this situation, Hezekiah. I'll take care of it Myself."Then He sent His angel out, killed 145,000 Assyrian soldiers and sent the Assyrian king home in fear. Once there, he was killed by his own sons and, of course, never troubled Judah again.

That's a wonderful end to the story, don't you think? But it might not have turned out as wonderfully if Hezekiah hadn't known how to wait on the Lord. If He had been like many Christians today, he might have rushed into his prayer room and started firing off prayers like a machine gun. He might have started shouting, "LORD, I KNOW YOU SAID YOU'D ALWAYS LEAD US IN TRIUMPH, SO I'M JUST GOING TO MARCH OUR ARMY OUT THERE AND FIGHT THOSE ASSYRIANS. I'M PRAYING THE PRAYER OF FAITH RIGHT NOW BELIEVING THAT YOU'LL GIVE US THE STRENGTH TO CONQUER THEM. I BELIEVE I RECEIVE— AMEN!"

Although that sounds like a very fine prayer, it would have been the wrong prayer because it would have been contrary to God's plan.

You see, it wasn't enough for Hezekiah to know God would give them victory. He also needed to know what he should do to receive that victory. And in this case, it was to do absolutely nothing but trust God.

Many times when we face situations where we sense God speaking to us but we don't yet have all the answers we need from Him, we should do what Hezekiah did. Instead of just spouting prayers in every direction, we should lay our problem before the Lord. Then we look to Him to reveal not only His will but His way. We should wait patiently until He shows us exactly how to pray.

Give God Time to Speak

I encountered a serious situation like that just a few years ago. The Lord spoke to my heart and told me to set aside all ministry activities and devote my time exclusively to prayer. It was easier said than done. I am a pastor's wife. I do some of the preaching and teaching at our church. My husband feels strongly that I'm called to do those things and he depends on me to help him.

So I went to the Lord with those problems. I said, "Father, if this is truly Your will, I need You to show me what I should do about these other responsibilities. I'll need You to speak to my husband and help him understand." In a very simple way, I laid out the difficulties before Him. Then I simply waited in worship and in fellowship with Him.

Over the next several days as I continued to wait on God, the Holy Spirit began to show me how to pray about the matter. He led me to lay my motives on the altar before the Lord, to pray the prayer of consecration and say, "Lord, I just want Your will in my life. I want to do exactly what You want me to do." He led me to pray in tongues and in other ways. Then one day, the Lord came to me in a great visitation. He helped me know what I was to do, how I was to do it and He filled me with such a great assurance of His will that I never had to wonder about it again. Regardless of what people said to me, they couldn't shake me because I had received a clear revelation of God's will in my spirit.

This is where so many Christians miss the will of God for their lives. Instead of waiting on Him, they just try to figure out in their brains what the best course of action would be. The problem is, God's plan for us isn't in our brains. It's in our hearts! And if we want to know what that plan is, we must allow the Holy Spirit to bring it up from our hearts and reveal it to us in times of quiet waiting.

"But I can't spend eight hours a day waiting on the Lord!"

You don't have to. You might just wait on Him about a certain issue for 15 or 20 minutes, then go on your way. Later in the day you might spend another 15 minutes waiting, minutes you otherwise might have spent talking on the phone or watching television. You'll be amazed at what you can hear from God in just those brief moments.

Even if you aren't facing a big decision, spend time waiting on the Lord anyway. Give Him time to speak to you about the small things in your life because they often make a much bigger difference than you might think. Walking in God's perfect plan is like baking a cake. You can put in all the major ingredients, but if you leave out a pinch of this or a handful of that, it won't turn out right. That's why Ephesians 5:15 says, "Look carefully then how you walk! Live purpose fully and worthily and accurately..."

Often what God wants to do during your times of waiting on Him and seeking His face is simply to bring your thinking up to His level. He wants to lift your faith sites higher so He can bless you not according to your puny, natural thinking, but according to His riches in glory.

Some years ago a Christian businessman who is a millionaire several times over told me that the Lord spoke to him and said, "My son, you wouldn't have a measly few million dollars if you had My thinking. You'd be worth 50 million by now if you'd spent more time listening to Me."

You are changed when you wait in the presence of God. Your thinking is changed and as a result your body is changed; your finances are changed; your life is changed. I think those kinds of changes are worth the wait, don't you?

CHAPTER 10

The Powerful Practice of Praise

Bless the Lord, O my soul: and all that is within me, bless his holy name. Bless the Lord, O my soul, and forget not all his benefits. (Psalms 103:1-2 KJV)

The fourth and final prayer habit I will mention here is the habit of praising and worshipping God. I cannot leave it out because it is a must for every person who is serious about prayer. The reason is simple. As we have already noted, the manifest presence of God is a necessity if we are to sense His leadership as we pray. And since God inhabits the praises of His people (Psalm 22:3), we would be wise to make praise a continual practice in our house of prayer.

Actually, the failure to worship is the cause behind much of our powerlessness in prayer. Many people don't understand that. They think that God's ways are so mysterious that prayer must always be a hit or miss proposition. "Sometimes God sends His power and sometimes He doesn't," they say. "You never know what He is going to do."

But the the Bible tells us differently. It says we are meant to know and understand "the exceeding greatness of [God's] power toward us who believe" (Ephesians 1:19 KJV).

You see, there are laws that govern the supernatural realm just as there are laws that govern the natural operations of this earth. If you understand and operate according to those laws, you can consistently tap into God's power. The truth is, if you're a Christian, you've already discovered how to do it in at least one area. You've learned how to operate the law which governs the power of God for salvation.

If thou shalt confess with thy mouth the Lord Jesus, and shalt believe in thine heart that God hath raised him from the dead, thou shalt be saved. For with the heart man believeth unto righteousness; and with the mouth confession is made unto salvation.
(Romans 10:9-10 KJV)

Once you discovered God's power for salvation was available to all who would believe in their hearts and confess with their mouths, you put that law into action and you were born again. Would the same law work for anyone else who sincerely applied it? Certainly it would!

As you can see from that example, God's power takes different forms. Sometimes it brings the new birth. At other times the Word of God describes it as bringing light and life (John 1:4-5). It can also bring the anointing for healing, deliverance (Acts 10:38), or the glory (Romans 6:4). But no matter what form God's power takes, one thing remains true—it is "to us-ward" as Ephesians 1:19 says. In other words, He is constantly sending it our way.

The reason we see so little of it is not because God is withholding it from us. He isn't sitting up in heaven saying, "I'm almighty God. I possess great power and you can't have any of it." He wants us to have it. He has even given us the Bible to show us how to tap into it. The cause for our power failures in prayer lies with us, not with Him.

One of the laws that brings God's power into action in our lives is the law of praise and worship. We can see that law in operation all through the Bible. One of the most dramatic examples is found in 2 Chronicles 5. There we find that during the dedication of Solomon's temple...

> *...when the trumpeters and singers were*
> *joined in unison, making one sound to be*
> *heard in praising and thanking the Lord,*
> *and when they lifted up their voice with the*
> *trumpets and cymbals and other instru-*
> *ments for song and praised the Lord, saying,*
> *For He is good; for His mercy and loving-*
> *kindness endure forever, then the house of*
> *the Lord was filled with a cloud, so that the*
> *priests could not stand to minister because*
> *of the cloud, for the glory of the Lord filled*
> *the house of God.* (verses 13-14)

As these people began to enter into true worship, a spiritual law was put to work and immediately God's power was released in their midst. In this particular instance, the power came in the form of a glory cloud that literally knocked the priests off their feet. In Acts 13, we can see it manifest in a different form. There we see certain prophets and teachers from the church at Antioch, along with Saul of Tarsus, gathering for a real Holy Spirit-led meeting.

> *As they ministered to the Lord, and fasted,*
> *the Holy Ghost said, Separate me Barnabas*
> *and Saul for the work whereunto I have*
> *called them. And when they had fasted and*
> *prayed, and laid their hands on them and*
> *sent them away. So they, being sent forth by*
> *the Holy Ghost, departed...* (verses 2-4 KJV)

In this case the power came forth in the form of clear direction from God and an anointing so strong that from then on, Saul became known as the apostle Paul, perhaps the most powerful and effective minister of the Gospel this world has ever seen with the exception of Jesus Himself.

How did the believers at Antioch tap into such great power? They did it through ministering to the Lord, which is another term for waiting and worshipping, and you can do it the same way.

Think of it like this. Just as your city has a huge generator that supplies electricity you can tap into by simply plugging in a cord, God has a similar system. His throne is like a huge, spiritual generator from which the river of life flows. (See Revelation 22:1.) As we worship, we plug into that generator and power (or life) begins to flow in us. That's why God wants us to worship—not because He needs us to make Him feel good about Himself but because He wants us to plug into His power!

You're always plugged in somewhere. In fact, you're plugged into something right now. You might be plugged into what your mind is thinking. You might be plugged into your circumstances. If you're sick, you might be plugged into your doctor's diagnosis. But if you want to get the power of God flowing, you'll have to unplug from those places and plug yourself into the throne of God through praise.

Please understand, however, when I say *praise*, I'm not talking about the absent-minded religious rituals that so often pass for praise and worship among Christians today. I'm talking about true worship, the kind John 4:23 says comes from true (genuine) worshippers who "will worship the Father in spirit and in truth (reality); for the Father is seeking just such people as these as His worshipers."

We can (and often do) act like we're worshipping when we're not truly worshipping at all. We can go into our place of prayer, shut our eyes and raise our hands when all the while we're thinking, *Hmmmm, I wonder what I should cook for dinner tonight?* Or we might be saying, "Thank you, Jesus. Thank you. Praise...praise...praise." But if we're just repeating those words mechanically without giving them much thought or meaning, we're not worshipping in truth. We're not being real with God; we're just being religious.

If your husband or wife did something nice for you and you appreciated it, you wouldn't just go to them and say, "Oh, thank you, thank you...praise, praise praise." No, you'd tell them specifically what you were thanking them for. You'd say, for example, "Thank you so much for cleaning up the dishes last night. I was so tired and your help was a great blessing."

If you want to truly worship the Lord, you need to be real with Him in the same way. Has He done anything good for you? Then worship Him for it. Tell Him how much you appreciate the fact that He saved you, that He rescued you from darkness and brought you into His Light. If He has healed your body, tell Him how grateful you are for it. If He has set you free from some kind of bondage, thank Him for giving you that freedom.

Praise and worship Him for who He is. Say, "Jesus, I thank You for being my Friend. I praise You that You'll never leave me and You'll never forsake me. Oh Jesus, I've given You opportunity to stop loving me, but You never have and I'm so grateful."

You can also take scripture promises that are especially meaningful to you and praise Him with them. Worship Him for being the God who supplies all your needs according to His riches in glory (Philippians 4:19). Praise Him for being your Shepherd and leading you in the paths of righteousness (Psalm 23:1-2). Thank Him for putting His own Holy Spirit inside you to teach you and help you in every situation (John 14:17).

But always remember this, if you want to be a true worshipper, you can't be lazy in your worship. You can't let it consist only of light, frivolous phrases you toss out without much thought. You must reach down into your heart and bring up something for which you're really grateful.

You might just start with one little thing, but as you offer it up to God with a sincere heart, something supernatural will happen. The Bible talks about it in Hebrews 13:15. There it says, "Through Him, therefore, let us constantly and at all times offer up to God a sacrifice of praise, which is the fruit of lips that thankfully acknowledge and confess and glorify His name."

Since that scripture says praise is in order constantly, or at all times, you can never go wrong praising God. So if you start to pray and can't seem to locate your heart and sense which direction God wants you to go, you can always lift your heart in genuine worship. It will get you moving in the right direction.

Also, notice the first three words in that verse, *Through Him, therefore.* They indicate we don't have to worship by our own strength alone. We can do it through Him. As we begin to lift up our hearts in worship, the Holy Ghost will help us. He will inspire us with truth.

As you begin by speaking one truth out to God, He'll bring another truth right up out of your spirit. As you continue, He'll keep bringing up more and more truth until your heart pours forth in full and genuine worship. Sometimes I compare the process to drilling for oil. You keep reaching down into your heart deeper and deeper until you finally hit a gusher.

When that happens, you'll be worshipping both in *spirit* and in *truth*. What's more, you'll be plugged into God's own generator and you'll experience the unlimited, surpassingly great power God longs to pour out on us who believe. That's the kind of power you need to pray effectively, so don't wait for the Sunday morning worship service to tap into it. You don't need a music director or a song sheet to worship. All you need is a heart of love for God and a mouth ready to speak His praises.

So establish the habit of worship in your house of prayer and plug into the power today!

CHAPTER 11

Taking Your Cues

*But now we are discharged from the Law
and have terminated all intercourse with it,
having died to what once restrained and
held us captive. So now we serve not under
[obedience to] the old code of written regula-
tions, but [under obedience to the prompt-
ings] of the Spirit in newness of life.*
(Romans 7:6)

As you begin to establish good prayer habits in your life and cultivate a consciousness of the Holy Spirit working within you, you'll be ready to take your cues. When I say *cues*, I'm talking about those gentle promptings of the Holy Spirit that come to you, not only in your special prayer times but throughout the day.

I refer to them as cues because they remind me of the cards used by the television crew to help Mac and me when we're taping TV broadcasts. When we need to be reminded of the time, or we need to say something particular, they flash a little card our way. We'll see it for just a moment, then it's gone.

Whether you realize it or not, the Holy Spirit works in much the same manner with you. You'll be driving down the street just fellowshipping with Him when suddenly someone will flash across your mind. You'll think, *My lands, I haven't seen that person in years. I wonder what made me think of them?*

Come on, get a clue! It was the Holy Spirit and He wasn't bringing that person to your mind just so you could think about them. Thinking about people doesn't help them. No, when the Holy Spirit gives you such promptings He is wanting you to pray.

Because we haven't realized that, we've all missed countless opportunities. We've had times when a specific person would be on our mind on and off for days. Then shortly thereafter, we might hear he was hurt in a car accident. So we'd visit him in the hospital and say, "Bless your heart, I've just been thinking and thinking about you." If we had taken our cue and prayed, he probably wouldn't be in the hospital at all!

"Sister Hammond," you ask, "are you saying I could save someone from harm or disaster just by praying one simple prayer?"

Yes! In fact, I remember one time in particular when one of the praying women at our church did exactly that. She prayed for a lady the Lord brought to mind one day then jotted her a note to let her know she'd prayed for her. As it turned out on the very day she prayed, the lady was hit by a car. Instead of being seriously hurt, she ended up with just a sprained ankle!

Many times we overlook such promptings to pray because we don't realize how supernatural they are. We expect supernatural things to be more spectacular. We're waiting to see stars or to have an angel appear to us and say in a thundering voice, "I WANT YOU TO PRAY FOR SO-AND-SO!"

But most of the time, that's not how the Holy Spirit works. He just gives us an impression, quietly speaks a name to our heart, or flashes someone's face before us. Often, His promptings are so light and gentle that if you aren't looking for them, you'll either miss them altogether or mistake them for something natural.

The reason it seems so natural is because, spiritually speaking, it is. If you're born again and baptized in the Holy Spirit, it is completely natural for you to be receiving impressions or transmissions from the Holy Spirit. After all, He is living inside you. And He isn't just sitting around in there. He's at work, doing what Jesus said He would do— bringing things to your remembrance, revealing and disclosing the things of God, helping you to pray as you ought.

He doesn't just do those things sporadically, either. He does them all the time! The more you train yourself to listen to your heart, the more you'll hear His voice. He'll send you cues as fast as you can catch them because He is the Spirit of grace and supplication. He is always ready to pray! He is there to empower us to "pray without ceasing" (1 Thessalonians 5:17).

Little Prayers Can Make a Big Difference

Of course, we don't have to get in our prayer closet and stay all day long on our knees to be constant in prayer. As we go about the daily affairs of life, we can be yielding ourselves to the Holy Spirit. We can be listening to our hearts, catching our cues and lifting them up to the Lord in prayer.

It's amazing what the Holy Ghost can accomplish through the simple little prayers we pray in the ordinary course of a day. They can literally save lives. I know that from personal experience.

Some years ago, I was standing in my kitchen whipping potatoes for supper when Mac came to my mind. No spiritual fireworks went off. No writing from God appeared on the wall. I just had a gentle sensing, an impression that Mac was in danger. So what did I do? Did I just have warm feelings toward him and think, *Oh, poor Mac, he's in danger.*

No, I began to pray whatever came to my heart. First, I pled the blood of Jesus over him for protection. Then as I prayed in tongues and yielded to the promptings of the Spirit, I began to pray some unusual things about his airplane. Although Mac is a pilot, I didn't know he was flying that day. But as I followed the leadership of the Holy Spirit, I began to pray about the wheels on his plane.

I never did experience a great sense of urgency. I simply took my cues, prayed until I sensed a release in my heart and then went on about my business.

When Mac came home that night I said, "What on earth happened to you today?"

He told me he'd taken another fellow up in his plane to show him some things about instrument flying and when they started to land, the landing gear malfunctioned. He had to "belly in" which is very dangerous. Mac is an excellent pilot, however, and everything went alright until the plane hit a rise at the end of the runway which caused it to tilt to one side and catch one of the wings on the ground.

"I just knew the plane was about to start rolling," Mac said. "But then the most amazing thing happened. As soon as we started to flip, it was as if something picked the plane up, straightened it out on the runway and set it down safe and sound."

As you can imagine, when I heard that I was certainly glad I yielded to the Holy Spirit's prompting to pray that afternoon!

It's interesting to me that in spite of the seriousness of the situation, it just took a few minutes of Spirit-led prayer to take care of it. In many instances, that's the way it is. You don't always have to drop what you're doing, fall down on your knees and pray for hours when you sense a prompting from God. Quite often you'll just pray briefly and that's all you'll need to do.

You Are God's Mouthpiece

Some people have gotten off into extremes thinking we must always labor and travail if God is to work powerfully in a situation. But that's just not true. When the apostle Paul wrote to the churches at Rome, Ephesus and Thessalonica, he said he "made mention" of them often in his prayers. Do you think God moved in those churches in response to those brief prayers Paul lifted up on their behalf? Certainly He did!

When you're praying according to the direction of the Holy Spirit, you're speaking God's Words and His Words make things happen. All He had to say was, "Let there be light," and a darkness so great it had engulfed this entire earth was conquered in an instant.

God's Words are containers of His power. But since He has given mankind dominion over the earth, in order to release His power into people's lives, He needs a man or a woman to speak His Words for Him. He needs someone to be His mouthpiece.

That's what you're doing when you're driving down the street in your car just taking your little cues. You're making yourself available to God. You're opening the way for Him to intervene in situations by speaking His Word over them. Sometimes you'll be able to accomplish the Holy Spirit's desire for someone by simply mentioning them once or twice in prayer. At other times, the Lord will continue to bring the person to your heart and those initial cues will begin to grow stronger. You'll sense a flow of love and mercy drawing you toward that person and you'll know they need further attention in prayer.

God so intensely desires to pour out His mercy on people, He'll prompt you to pray for people you don't even know. That happened to me a few months before the Gulf War. The Holy Spirit had repeatedly brought the name *Guy Hunter* to my mind. I'd never heard of Guy Hunter and I had no understanding of how to pray for him so I'd just lift his name up before the Lord and pray in tongues.

Eventually, however, I began to see things in my spirit when I would pray for him. I'd see him crouched down in some kind of box. The heat was coming down on that box and he was about to suffocate. So I prayed Psalm 91 over him fervently asking for the protection of God on his behalf.

One morning just after the Gulf War began, I turned on the television and heard the newscasters talking about the prisoners of war who had been taken captive. One of the pilots mentioned was Guy Hunter! When I heard that I just said, "Glory to God!" because I knew he'd be all right. I'd been praying for him all summer.

Get Started!

Some people think God moves in such miraculous ways for me because I have a special call to pray. But remember, the Bible says "He Who supplies you with His marvelous [Holy] Spirit...works powerfully and miraculously among you...because of your believing" (Galatians 3:5).

Notice that scripture doesn't say the Holy Spirit will work miraculously with you if you have a special call to pray. It doesn't say He'll do it if you're a very mature Christian who fasts every week and spends six hours a day in the prayer closet. It says He'll work powerfully and miraculously with you because of your believing.

So, just believe and trust God to help you follow the promptings of the Holy Spirit and He will work powerfully and miraculously in your prayer life just as He does in mine.

Does that mean you'll be able to wake up tomorrow morning and instantly start picking up every cue the Holy Spirit sends your way? Probably not. I've been practicing this lifestyle of prayer for more than 20 years now and I've found it takes time for God to develop you in it.

There is something, however, you *can* do right away. You can get started. You can begin to teach yourself to walk with a consciousness of God. You can start training yourself to listen to your heart throughout the day so you don't miss the cues the Holy Spirit is sending you. At first, you may only think about it a couple of times a day. But stay with it, keep trusting God and you'll get better at it every day.

In addition, begin studying and meditating what the Bible has to say about the work of the Holy Spirit. I know I've mentioned that before, but it's so important it's worth repeating. You see, it doesn't matter how much you've studied the Word in that area if you want to keep expanding your ability to work with the Holy Spirit, you need to keep on studying.

Jesus said, "The measure [of thought and study] you give [to the truth you hear] will be the measure [of virtue and knowledge] that comes back to you" (Mark 4:24). The word *virtue* actually means *power*. So if you want to increase your power to pray by the Spirit, keep increasing in God's Word.

As you begin to pick up your cues, don't be discouraged if they don't seem particularly exciting or dramatic. Despite the striking prayer experiences I've shared with you in these pages, you can be sure the cues I receive don't all involve plane crashes or unknown P.O.W.'s. Most of them seem very ordinary, and in many cases I never find out what happened as a result of my prayers. But it doesn't matter. I just keep praying by faith, lifting up those things the Holy Spirit puts in my heart, confidently believing each and every one is extremely important to God.

Prayer Begins With God

Do you know why those little cues are so important to Him? Because they come from His heart.

It's vital for us to understand that. You see, true prayer never starts with us. It always starts with God. It is a cycle that begins when He puts His thoughts and ways into our heart.

Isaiah 55 tells us how to set that cycle in motion.

Seek ye the Lord while he may be found, call
ye upon him while he is near: let the wicked

*forsake his way, and the unrighteous man
his thoughts: and let him return unto the
Lord, and he will have mercy upon him;
and to our God, for he will abundantly pardon. For my thoughts are not your thoughts,
neither are your ways my ways, saith the
Lord. For as the heavens are higher than the
earth, so are my ways higher than your
ways, and my thoughts than your thoughts.
For as the rain cometh down, and the snow
from heaven, and returneth not thither, but
watereth the earth, and maketh it bring
forth and bud, that it may give seed to the
sower, and bread to the eater: so shall my
word be that goeth forth out of my mouth:
it shall not return unto me void, but it shall
accomplish that which I please, and it shall
prosper in the thing whereto I sent it.*
(verses 6-11 KJV)

When we forsake wickedness and our own ways, and we begin to seek God through His Word and through prayer, something wonderful happens. God begins to take the desires, dreams and plans that are in His heart and put them into our heart.

Why does He do that? Because to bring those things forth in the earth, He needs someone to lift them up to Him in prayer. He needs someone to ask Him for them. Therefore He works "in you both to will and to do of his good pleasure" (Philippians 2:13 KJV), causing His desires to become your desires too.

When those desires first manifest in the form of promptings or cues, they may seem ever so slight. In those early stages, I liken them to seeds God has planted in your heart. Some seeds are like avocado seeds. They're big enough to be immediately recognized and prayed for properly. But other seeds are like marigold seeds, hardly more than a speck. So, as you lift them up to God, He receives them, and sends them back to you in a bigger, stronger form.

Here's how the cycle works. One day, you might just be spending some quiet time with the Lord, waiting on Him and fellowshipping with Him, when you begin to sense a prompting to pray for a particular nation. Naturally speaking, you may not care anything about that nation. You might not even know anyone of that nationality. But that doesn't matter because the prompting for that nation isn't originating with you. It is coming from the heart of God for as 2 Peter 3:9 says, He is not willing that any should perish.

When you first notice the desire stirring within you, it may seem to be little more than a vague inclination. But as you continue to respond to the Spirit's promptings they will grow stronger. Eventually you may find yourself in the grip of such a fervent desire for that nation to be saved you begin to weep over it.

Yet even as you are weeping, you can be rejoicing because you know the "fervent prayer...availeth much" (James 5:16). The prayer that is backed by God's own desire is sure to be answered.

I believe Jesus was referring primarily to those kinds of desires when He said, "What things soever ye desire, when ye pray, believe that ye receive them, and ye shall have them" (Mark 11:24 KJV). People often interpret that scripture in such a superficial fashion. They think, *Isn't that wonderful! God is going to give me every quirky little thing I want if I'll just believe I'll receive it.*

Of course there's nothing wrong with having your own personal desires and expecting God as a loving Father to grant them. But the deeper you go in your relationship with Him, the less you'll find yourself praying about those things and the more you'll find yourself praying about the much more significant desires that come to you from the throne of God.

It is important to note that although you can have an abundance of prayer seeds in your heart, you cannot bring them all to the point of harvest at once. Thus, you must bring them forth as God leads, one by one. As a result, your prayer life will change from time to time. You'll find yourself being led for months to pray for a certain situation or a certain person. But eventually, you'll bring that seed forth and be finished with it. Then you'll start working on another seed.

One thing is sure, God is an abundant supplier so you'll never run out of prayer seeds. If you choose to yield to the Holy Spirit, you'll be cultivating them and bringing them to harvest for the rest of your life.

Be Led by the Spirit—Not by Needs

I do want to warn you. As you follow the promptings of the Holy Spirit in your prayer life and allow Him to be your guide, you will not always be praying about those things that seem to your natural mind to be most in need of prayer. You won't always be praying about those urgent situations people say you should be focusing upon.

I can think of many such times in my own life. I remember days on end, for example, spent praying over the birth of someone's baby. Looking at the other more pressing issues around me I would wonder, *Why is God focusing so intently on this one little baby?*

Only God Himself knew the answer to that question. Only He knew the call of heaven on that child's life. My part was not to try to figure it out. It was simply to pray and obey.

In your life of prayer, there will also be times when instead of jumping on the bandwagon of busyness, the Spirit will lead you to be still and pray instead. Many people (not just heathens but good, God-loving Christians) won't understand. But you must determine in advance that no matter what others may say and do, you are going to follow the Word of God and unction of the Holy Spirit.

You see, there will always be more needs around you than you can possibly manage in prayer. When you wake up in the morning and turn on the news, you'll hear about dozens of urgent matters that seem to scream for prayer. When you go to church, you may be handed a list of dozens more who need prayer. Then a relative will call and tell you of several more family situations that demand prayer.

Given the hundreds of needs you encounter every day, how can you possibly know where to begin praying? How can you decide which are the most urgent? Perhaps there are some needs God is leading others to pray for. You could take those needs off your list if you only knew which ones they were. And what if there is a need far more important that should take first priority but it is as yet unknown to you? How can you pray for that?

Only by following the promptings of the Spirit. He is the only One who can rightly direct your prayers.

A Silly Waste...or a Good Work?

Some might say, "Well, it seems to me God has given us a mind so we can logically decide these things." But logic must base its judgments on what can be perceived by the senses, and the realms of God extend far beyond the natural world.

There is an incident recorded in Matthew 26 which demonstrates that fact quite clearly.

> *Now when Jesus was in Bethany, in the house of Simon the leper, there came unto him a woman having an alabaster box of very precious ointment, and poured it on his head, as he sat at meat. But when his disciples saw it, they had indignation, saying, To what purpose is this waste? For this ointment might have been sold for much, and given to the poor. When Jesus understood it, he said unto them, Why trouble ye the woman? for she hath wrought a good work upon me. For ye have the poor always with you; but me ye have not*

always. For in that she hath poured this oint-
ment on my body, she did it for my burial.
Verily I say unto you, Wheresoever this gospel
shall be preached in the whole world, there
shall also this, that this woman hath done, be
told for a memorial of her. (verses 6-13 KJV)

If you'll investigate the scriptures, you'll find the woman to whom this story refers is Mary, the sister of Lazarus and Martha. She was a very spiritual woman and more than once in the Bible we find her behaving in ways that to the natural mind seem peculiar or even inappropriate. In Luke 10, for instance, we find her sitting at the feet of Jesus listening to Him preach even though her sister, Martha, sorely needed her help to serve the guests in their house. To Martha (and no doubt to many today) Mary seemed to be shirking her Christian duty. After all, there was work to be done! Yet Jesus said she had made the proper choice by electing first to fellowship with Him and hear His Word.

Now here in Matthew 26, we find Mary once again offending the religious sensibilities of those around her as she pours perfume worth 300 denarii—a laboring man's wages for a year—upon the head of Jesus. Logically speaking, it does seem like a silly waste, doesn't it? Just think how many people could have been fed with that money! Think how many needs could have been met!

But Mary wasn't being led by needs, she was being led by the Holy Spirit. And He knew something no one else knew except Jesus Himself. He knew the crucifixion was coming. He knew it was the most important event ever to take place in the history of man. And He knew certain things must be done in preparation for it.

None of the people in Simon's house understood that—probably not even Mary herself. But she followed her heart and because she did so, Jesus said she would be remembered wherever the Gospel was preached.

That is a lesson every serious person of prayer must remember. We must realize we can't afford to be directed by outward appearances and opinions. We must be led by the Holy Spirit. He knows where our prayers are truly needed. If He leads us to pray about a situation, we cannot afford to ignore His leadership and spend our time doing other things or praying about things that seem to be more urgent. If the season to pray is now, we can't bring it back later. We must take the opportunities when the Spirit brings them, for if we miss them they'll be gone.

As you yield yourself to the Holy Spirit, there will be occasions when you can't go to the church picnic because you're being led to pray instead. There will be times when you will have to lay down your knife and fork, or pass up a trip to the mall. It may seem like a sacrifice at the time, but in the end you'll be so glad you made it.

For on that day when you stand before Jesus and He reveals the miracles that were wrought through your prayers, when He says to you as He said of Mary, "You have done a good work," you'll be ever so grateful that amid the clamoring needs and distractions of life you chose to follow Him.

CHAPTER 12

Stop, Look and Listen

But he that entereth in by the door is the shepherd of the sheep. To him the porter openeth; and the sheep hear his voice: and he calleth his own sheep by name, and leadeth them out. And when he putteth forth his own sheep, he goeth before them, and the sheep follow him: for they know his voice. (John 10:2-4 KJV)

Since only by discerning the direction of the Holy Spirit can we truly pray as we ought, it is essential for us to clearly understand how to follow His leadership. The best way to gain that understanding is by looking at the earthly ministry of Jesus. He is our example and we are to follow the Spirit in the same way He did.

In the fifth chapter of John, He revealed to us precisely the method He used.

*I assure you, most solemnly I tell you, the Son is able to do nothing of Himself (of His own accord); but He is able to do only **what He sees the Father doing**, for whatever the Father does is what the Son does in the same way [in His turn]. The Father dearly loves the Son and discloses to **(shows)** Him everything that He Himself does...I am able to do nothing from Myself [independently, of My own accord—but only as I am taught by God and as I get His orders]. Even **as I hear**, I judge [I decide as I am bidden to decide. **As the voice comes to Me**, so I give a decision]...*(verses 19-20, 30)

Again in John 8 He said:

*...He who sent Me is true (reliable), and I tell the world [only] the things that **I have heard** from Him...I tell the things which **I have seen** and learned at My Father's side.* (verses 26, 38)

If you'll examine those verses carefully, you'll find Jesus followed the leadership of the Holy Spirit by seeing and hearing. Not the kind done with physical eyes and ears, of course. That kind of seeing and hearing comes purely through human strength and Jesus said He did *nothing* of Himself. He was never directed by His flesh.

No, as Jesus went about His earthly life He couldn't see God with His physical eyes any more than you and I can. When He spoke of seeing and hearing, He was referring to that which is done in the realm of the spirit. And the scriptural fact is, if you are born again and baptized in the Holy Spirit you are just as well-equipped to see and hear in that realm as He was.

That may come as stunning news to you. But it is true, nonetheless. For even though Jesus is the divine Son of almighty God, when He came to earth He laid aside the privileges of His divinity. He took on human flesh with all its earthly limitations. (See Phillipians 2:5-7.)

He had to live by faith in the Word and not by sight (2 Corinthians 5:7). He had to be baptized in the Holy Spirit before He could minister in power (Matthew 3:16). He had to be led of the Spirit in everything He did (John 5:30).

After His crucifixion and resurrection, He ascended to the Father and sent the Holy Spirit back to us just as He had promised. Why? So the Spirit could lead us, empower us and in all ways do for us exactly what He did for Jesus!

Look again at what Jesus said to His disciples just before He went to the cross:

> *I have yet many things to say unto you, but ye cannot bear them now. Howbeit when he, the Spirit of truth, is come, he will guide you into all truth: for he shall not speak of himself; but whatsoever he shall hear, that shall he speak: and he will shew you things to come.* (John 16:12-13 KJV)

Now, let me ask you a very simple question. What happens when someone speaks to you? You hear them, right? If they speak to you physically, you hear them with your physical ears. By the same token, when the Holy Spirit speaks to you, you hear Him with the ears of your heart.

That's how you will know what to pray about certain situations. You'll hear words in your heart and you'll speak them out with your mouth.

At other times, the Holy Spirit will show you things (John 16:13). You'll see images—not with your physical eyes, but in your heart—or you'll have impressions. And with childlike simplicity, you'll just pray the things He shows you.

Don't Strain Your Brain

It is vital for you to remember, however, such seeing and hearing does not come through your own, fleshly efforts. It comes in response to your faith in God's Word.

After all, He's the One who said He would speak to you and show you things by the Holy Spirit. It's His responsibility to get the job done. He is big enough to do it too. So just trust Him. Believe Him to do whatever it takes to get His message through to you. Don't get tied up in knots of apprehension *trying* to see and hear. Relax and let the Spirit do His work in you.

It's amazing what He can accomplish if we'll stop trying so hard and just follow Him. I saw a particularly wonderful illustration of that a few years ago. I was counseling with a precious lady who had been through a terrible ordeal in her marriage. She desperately needed to be delivered from the pain she'd been through, but no matter how hard I tried I couldn't seem to help her. (That was the problem; *I* was trying to do it!)

One day as I was talking with her, I *heard* something. The Holy Spirit spoke James 5:13 to my heart. *"Is any among you afflicted?...let him pray."*

Well, we can certainly do that, I thought. So she and I began to lift our hearts to God. As we prayed, an image formed in my spirit. With the eyes of my heart, I could see this little lady twirling and dancing for joy. I could see her delivered!

I knew then, our work was done. I laughed and rejoiced, and sure enough, as we continued to pray she began to see it, too, and joined in my rejoicing. We knew we had the breakthrough because we had seen the wonderful deliverance God was about to perform in her life.

Isn't that delightfully simple? I love that about the Lord. He never complicates things. He doesn't give us complex instructions we can't follow. He always keeps things clean and simple.

What causes us to get confused is instead of just following Him like little children, obeying what we see and hear in our hearts, we try to figure everything out with our brains. I can tell you from experience, you'll never be able to do that with God. You'll never be able to understand why He tells you to do certain things in certain ways. So don't strain your brain trying. If you do, you're likely to come up with weird ideas that have nothing to do with spiritual reality.

I hate to think what strange theories I might have come up with if I had tried to figure out some of the cues God has given me over the years. There was a period of time some years ago when I kept seeing the letters RADZ as I prayed. It was as if I could see them printed on a page in a peculiar type-style. Of course, I had no idea what RADZ meant so I'd just say, "Lord, I lift up the RADZ to You."

At the time, we were believing God for a youth minister for our church. We knew exactly the kind of person we wanted and as the months went by, it seemed no one in the whole earth could fill the bill. Eventually, however, through a supernatural chain of events we met a young pastor from Louisiana named Steve. We liked him and thought he could be the one, but he wasn't at all interested in moving to Minneapolis.

All of us were praying and seeking God's direction on the matter. Then one day, I walked into Mac's office and on his desk lay a piece of paper. Printed there in the exact type-style I'd seen in my heart was the word RADZ. You can imagine how my spirit leapt!

"Mac," I asked, "what is this piece of paper here?"

"Oh, that's a flier Steve put together for a youth rally he wants to have. It's something about radical teens for Jesus. He calls them RADZ."

All that time, I had been praying for our new youth pastor and his ministry to our teenagers without even knowing it. How did I do it? Simply by praying what I saw in my heart. I didn't try to analyze it or figure it out. I just assumed God could reveal the meaning to me in His own time and His own way.

A Manifestation of Spiritual Gifts

"But I never see things like that when I pray!"

You will if you just keep meditating the Word and building your faith to flow in the Holy Ghost. In fact, you probably already have seen such things but you just weren't alert to them. They may have come so naturally you didn't recognize them for what they were—a manifestation of the gifts of the Holy Spirit.

First Corinthians 12 tells us about those gifts.

> *Now there are diversities of gifts, but the same Spirit. And there are differences of administrations, but the same Lord. And there are diversities of operations, but it is the same God which worketh all in all. But the manifestation of the Spirit is given to every man to profit withal. For to one is given by the Spirit the word of wisdom; to another the word of knowledge by the same Spirit; to another faith by the same Spirit; to another the gifts of healing by the same Spirit; to another the working of miracles; to another prophecy; to another discerning of spirits; to another divers kinds of tongues; to another the interpretation of tongues: but all these worketh that one and the selfsame Spirit, dividing to every man severally as he will.* (verses 4-11 KJV)

Even though the Bible says we should all "earnestly desire and cultivate" the gifts of the Spirit (1 Corinthians 14:1), most of us haven't developed them in our lives as we should. We've expected them to operate through the pastors and those in public ministry but not through us. It's time we changed that. It's time we started believing the Spirit will give His gifts to *every man*—just as He said He would!

We know, of course, He will not choose to use all of us in all the gifts during times of public ministry. He will divide them up so that we can operate together as a body. But in our own private lives, we can and should expect the Holy Spirit to help us by giving us whichever gift we need.

For example, when we don't know how to pray, we should expect the Holy Spirit to show and tell us things we could not otherwise know. Such revelations are actually manifestations of the word of knowledge or the word of wisdom operating within us. Often we don't recognize them as such because we think of the gifts as weird or extreme. We think when the word of knowledge comes to us it will be something like, "GO SPIT IN THE DIRT AND PUT MUD ON THAT BLIND MAN'S EYES SO HE'LL BE HEALED."

Listen, God is not going to start us out in our spiritual walk by telling us to spit on someone! He knows us too well. He knows if He told us to do something that radical we'd say, "No way!"

So what does He do instead? He gives us harmless little steps we can follow without getting too far out of our element. He shows us simple things to do and say in our prayer times so we can learn to obey Him without facing risks we're not spiritually mature enough to take.

One Step at a Time

In my own personal prayer times, I've often found He waits for me to act on the first thing He shows me before He'll give me any further direction. Sometimes when He wakes me in the night to pray, I'll say, "What is it, Lord?" Instead of hearing an answer, I'll see myself getting out of bed and going downstairs.

If I set aside that impression and stay in bed, I won't get anywhere in prayer. I might keep on asking, "Lord, what do you want me to pray about?" But every time I do, I'll just keep seeing myself getting out of bed and going downstairs. When I finally act on what I see and go downstairs, then and only then, will the Holy Spirit give me the next step.

I may never know why it was so important to the Lord for me to go downstairs. Often I think He is just training me to be obedient. He's helping me learn to flow with Him, so in times of emergency when someone's life depends on my ability to follow His directions, I'll be ready.

At those critical times, it usually requires more faith to be obedient to the Spirit's leadings and it helps if you've had plenty of practice. I remember one time in particular when that was true for me. I was at the bedside of my mother who was in the hospital dangerously ill. She had a brain aneurysm and was suffering seizures. When those seizures hit her, the demonic presence behind them was so strong it almost shook the room.

My sister and I had taken turns staying with her, making sure she was never alone. On about the fourth day, I was sitting in her room just waiting on the Lord because I didn't know what to do. (It doesn't do any good to strive and push your way through fleshly prayers. So when you haven't received revelation from the Lord about how to pray, the only thing you can do is be still and look to Him. You can't move until He moves.)

As I sat there, I *heard* the Holy Spirit speak down in my spirit. He said, "I want you to leave the hospital." Then I *saw* myself go to my sister's house and kneel on her bedroom floor.

Immediately, I began to argue. "Lord, you know I can't leave Mother now. She could die if I leave her." Of course, He didn't change His mind so I called my sister to the room and told her what I was going to do.

She was less than enthusiastic about the idea of being left alone at the hospital with Mother in such a critical state. "Why do you have to go to my house?" she asked. "Why can't you just pray here at the hospital like we've been doing for the past four days?"

"I don't know why," I answered. "I just know I have to do what the Holy Spirit is showing me."

She agreed and I went to her house. When I got there, I knelt on the bedroom floor just as I had envisioned. The moment I did, I began praying in other tongues. Then a most amazing thing happened. The Holy Spirit gave me the gift of discerning of spirits. In my heart I saw that a grotesque creature had wrapped itself around my mother, literally choking the life out of her. When I saw that image, I knew what to do. I commanded the creature to loose her and let her go. The whole process probably took less than 15 minutes but it broke the demonic power behind those seizures and within 24 hours they had stopped.

You know as well as I do, I could have never figured that out with my brain. I don't care how long I sat there and analyzed the situation, I never would have thought the solution lay in going to my sister's house and binding that devil on her bedroom floor. The only way to get answers in circumstances like that is to see, hear and obey one simple step at a time.

Three Ways to See

According to the Bible, there are three basic ways to see in the spirit. One is through a spiritual vision. That is a vision which, although not seen with your physical eyes, appears in distinct visual clarity to the eyes of your spirit.

You can find a scriptural example of such a vision in Acts 9. There we find Saul of Tarsus on his way to Damascus "breathing out threatenings and slaughter against the disciples of the Lord" (verse 1 KJV).

> *And as he journeyed, he came near Damascus: and suddenly there shined round about him a light from heaven: and he fell to the earth, and heard a voice saying unto him, Saul, Saul, why persecutest thou me? And he said, Who art thou, Lord? And the*

*Lord said, I am Jesus whom thou perse-
cutest: it is hard for thee to kick against the
pricks...And the men which journeyed with
him stood speechless, hearing a voice, but
seeing no man.* (verses 3-5, 7 KJV)

In this case, Saul was able to see Jesus yet we know He
was not openly visible because the men who were with Saul
saw *no man.* The Bible also tells us that Saul's eyes were
closed during this incident and "when his eyes were
opened...he was three days without sight" (verses 8, 9).
Therefore, we can be sure he was not seeing this vision with
his physical eyes. He was seeing the Lord with the eyes of
his spirit.

The second way to see spiritually is through an open
vision. That is a vision in which your eyes are open, you can
see your natural surroundings just as you normally would
but, at the same time, you can see images in the realm of
the spirit.

The apostle Peter had this particular type of vision in
Acts 10 when he went to the housetop to pray. Verse 11 says
"he saw heaven opened," and God proceeded to show him
things that would prepare him to set aside his religious tradi-
tions and preach the Gospel to the Gentiles.

The third and most common method of seeing is
through revelation. Revelation can come to you in a variety
of ways. As we've already discussed, it can come through
simple words of knowledge or wisdom from the Holy Spirit
in the form of promptings or impressions.

It can also come as you're listening to a sermon or
reading the Bible. Suddenly you will just see something you
never saw before. When I say you will *see* something, I don't
necessarily mean you had a visual image or a picture. I
mean you had a certain understanding or insight rise up
within you.

Another way revelation may come is through a shift in perspective. You might have been looking at a problem one way when all at once the Holy Spirit sheds a new light on it and you see the situation in an entirely different way. That often happens to me when I begin to fellowship with the Lord. His very presence changes the way I think and feel.

Psalm 73 provides a wonderful example of such a shift in perspective. There we can see the psalmist Asaph suffering from a deep sense of oppression as he begins his prayer to the Lord. He is so dismayed by the apparent prosperity and well-being of the wicked people around him, he is about to come to the conclusion that it's useless to serve God. He says:

> *They [the wicked] are not in trouble as other*
> *men; neither are they plagued like other*
> *men...Their eyes stand out with fatness: they*
> *have more than heart could wish. They are*
> *corrupt, and speak wickedly concerning*
> *oppression: they speak loftily. They set their*
> *mouth against the heavens, and their*
> *tongue walketh through the earth...And they*
> *say, How doth God know? and is there*
> *knowledge in the most High? Behold, these*
> *are the ungodly, who prosper in the world;*
> *they increase in riches. Verily I have cleansed*
> *my heart in vain, and washed my hands in*
> *innocency. For all the day long have I been*
> *plagued, and chastened every morning.*
> *When I thought to know this, it was too*
> *painful for me.* (verses 5-16 KJV)

Poor Asaph! He is really in a black mood, isn't he? Everywhere he looks he sees trouble and injustice. Things are so bad it hurts him even to think about them. There seemed to be no way out...

*Until I went into the sanctuary of God; then
understood I their end. Surely thou didst set
them in slippery places: thou castedst them
down into destruction. How are they
brought into desolation, as in a moment!
they are utterly consumed with terrors...So
foolish was I, and ignorant: I was as a beast
before thee. Nevertheless I am continually
with thee: thou hast holden me by my right
hand. Thou shalt guide me with thy counsel,
and afterward receive me to glory...My flesh
and my heart faileth: but God is the strength
of my heart, and my portion for ever.* (verses
17-19, 22-24, 26 KJV)

My, what a change in perspective! One moment,
Asaph was crying about how blessed the wicked were and
how miserable he was...and the next moment he was crow-
ing about how doomed the wicked were and how blessed
he was. What made the difference? He went into the sanctuary and the Spirit of God gave Him a revelation that
changed the way he saw his situation.

Suddenly, he was able to look beyond the present
moment. By the Holy Spirit he saw things to come. He
saw the eventual destruction of the ungodly. He saw the
goodness of God extending to him not just in this lifetime,
but forever!

I don't know about you, but I often need the Holy
Spirit to do for me what He did for Asaph. When I start feeling persecuted and overwhelmed, when all I want to do is
complain to God about the way I've been mistreated, I need
Him to open my eyes so I can see things from His heavenly,
eternal perspective instead of my limited, earthly one.

How do I get Him to do that? I just ask Him.

That's so simple, isn't it? Yet it amazes me how many
times we don't think to do it. We thrash around in our own
strength, trying to figure out our problems, striving to

improve our attitude—and failing. When all the while, the Holy Spirit is there inside us, ready and willing to help us, waiting for us to ask and believe, so He can show us things in a whole new light.

CHAPTER 13

A Scriptural Look at the Gift of Tongues

*For he that speaketh in an unknown
tongue speaketh not unto men, but unto
God: for no man understandeth him; howbeit in the spirit he speaketh mysteries.*
(1 Corinthians 14:2 KJV)

Sadly enough, many people in the Church today have deprived themselves of one of the most precious and powerful tools of prayer God has ever given us: the gift of tongues.

Some of them have been misled by well-meaning theologians who taught that tongues were no longer necessary in our day and therefore had passed away. Others have recognized tongues as a valid scriptural gift but have mistakenly thought it is given only to a rare and privileged few; and since those few are selected sovereignly by God, there is nothing average Christians can do to obtain it.

If you are among those precious believers who have fallen prey to such unscriptural ideas, I must be frank with you. You absolutely cannot afford to believe them any longer—especially if you're hungry to live a life of prayer.

"But Sister Lynne," you may say, "I'm just not comfortable with the gift of tongues. I haven't been raised to believe in it. Isn't it possible for me to pray without it?"

It is possible. But let me ask you this. Would a soldier step into battle with one hand voluntarily tied behind his back? Would he leave part of his weaponry at home? Certainly not. Yet that is what we do when we try to fulfill God's call to pray at this critical hour without availing ourselves of the gift of tongues.

What Does the Bible Say?

The only commentary on tongues (or any other issue) that can be fully trusted is the Bible itself. So, let's take a look at what it says.

Jesus Himself was the first to introduce the subject of tongues and He did so on the heels of what we have come to call the Great Commission. That was no coincidence, for whatever God calls us to do, He also equips us to do. And tongues is an essential piece of divine equipment for all of us who live in this New Testament dispensation.

> *And (Jesus) said unto them, Go ye into all the world, and preach the gospel to every creature. He that believeth and is baptized shall be saved; but he that believeth not shall be damned. And these signs shall follow them that believe; in my name shall they cast out devils; they shall speak with new tongues; they shall take up serpents; and if they drink any deadly thing, it shall not hurt them; they shall lay hands on the sick and they shall recover.* (Mark 16:15-18 KJV)

Notice the only qualification Jesus gives for speaking with new tongues is believing. He doesn't put time limits on that believing. He doesn't say, "He that believes over the next 30 or 40 years before tongues passes away." He simply says,

"Those who believe shall speak with new tongues."

Some have said this speaking with new tongues refers only to a more gracious type of speech (i.e. instead of cursing and using foul language, Christians would speak words of praise to God). Such an interpretation, however, requires us to take the phrase completely out of context. Every other sign Jesus lists in this passage is a supernatural sign, a wonder only God's mighty power could produce. It does not take supernatural power to refrain from using profanity. It only takes a strong will or a powerful enough deterrent (as any child who has had his mouth washed out with soap can testify).

To find out just how supernatural tongues are meant to be, we only have to move forward to the second chapter of Acts and see what happened ten days after Jesus made this proclamation. There we see the disciples gathered in prayer, awaiting the baptism of the Holy Spirit the Lord had promised them (Acts 1:5).

> *And when the day of Pentecost was fully come, they were all with one accord in one place. And suddenly there came a sound from heaven as of a rushing mighty wind, and it filled all the house where they were sitting. And there appeared unto them cloven tongues like as of fire, and it sat upon each of them. And they were all filled with the Holy Ghost, and began to speak with other tongues, as the Spirit gave them utterance. And there were dwelling at Jerusalem Jews, devout men, out of every nation under heaven. Now when this was noised abroad, the multitude came together, and were confounded, because that every man heard them speak in his own language. And they were all amazed and marvelled, saying one to another, Behold, are not all these which*

*speak Galilaeans? And how hear we every
man in our own tongue, wherein we were
born? Parthians, and Medes, and Elamites,
and the dwellers in Mesopotamia, and in
Judaea, and Cappadocia, in Pontus, and
Asia, Phyrgia, and Pamphilia, in Egypt and
in the parts of Libya about Cyrene, and
strangers of Rome, Jews and proselytes,
Cretes and Arabians, we do hear them speak
in our tongues the wonderful works of God.*
(verses 2:1-11 KJV)

As we can see here, tongues is a vocal miracle. It is a
language unknown to the speaker yet given to him by the
supernatural power of God. Sometimes it is an earthly language; other times it is a heavenly language. In 1 Corinthians
13:1 KJV, the apostle Paul referred to such supernatural
languages as "the tongues of men and of angels..." At
Pentecost it appears the tongues given the disciples were
tongues of men because the people of various languages
who were listening understood them.

Lest you think that incident was just an outstanding
display given by God to mark the beginning of the Holy
Ghost's dispensation and never to be repeated, let me assure
you it has happened in varying degrees countless times
since. One remarkable occurrence took place in Topeka,
Kansas, just after the turn of this century. A group of believers had gathered there under the leadership of Charles
Parham to seek God for the baptism of the Holy Ghost with
the evidence of speaking in other tongues.

At a little past midnight on January 1, 1901, a woman
by the name of Agnes Osman received it. For three days and
three nights she spoke in perfect Chinese, although she had
no prior knowledge of the language. She even wrote in
Chinese, a fact verified by a linguist who read what she had
written. Her experience marked the beginning of the
Pentecostal movement we know today.

Less spectacular, but exciting to me nevertheless, was an experience I had with that particular manifestation of tongues just a few years ago. Mac and I were participating in an ordination service for our missionaries to Peru. As we laid hands on them and separated them to the ministry to which God had called them, I began to pray in tongues. Although I don't know a word of Spanish, those missionaries later told me later I had prayed in perfect Spanish about their upcoming ministry in Peru. As a result, they were greatly encouraged.

The Initial Evidence of the Baptism in the Holy Spirit

Another thing we can see from the experience of the disciples at Pentecost is that tongues is the initial evidence of the baptism in the Holy Ghost. Some people claim it isn't and point to John the Baptist as proof. "He was full of the Holy Ghost," they say, "and he didn't speak with tongues."

That's true, but John the Baptist was a prophet who ministered under the Old Covenant. The gift of tongues is a unique gift given to New Covenant believers. That truth emerges again and again in the book of Acts. There we see five different instances in which tongues accompanied the baptism in the Holy Spirit in the early Church. And since the early Church is the example we are to follow—not Old Covenant prophets—we would do well to take a closer look at what happened there.

We have already examined the first incidence of tongues in the early Church. So let's look now at a second found in Acts 10. There we see Peter at the home of Cornelius, preaching the Gospel to the Gentiles for the first time.

While Peter yet spake these words, the Holy
Ghost fell on all them which heard the word.
And they of the circumcision which believed
were astonished, as many as came with

Peter, because that on the Gentiles also was poured out the gift of the Holy Ghost. For they heard them speak with tongues, and magnify God...(verses 44-46 KJV)

How did the Jewish disciples know the Holy Ghost had been poured out on the Gentiles? They spoke with tongues. That was the evidence.

In Acts 19 yet another such instance is recorded. In this case, the apostle Paul had stumbled upon a group of believers in Ephesus who, although they had received John's baptism, had not yet heard the full gospel. According to verses 2-6 KJV:

He [Paul] said unto them, Have ye received the Holy Ghost since ye believed? And they said unto him, We have not so much as heard whether there be any Holy Ghost. And he said unto them, Unto what then were ye baptized? And they said, Unto John's baptism. Then said Paul, John verily baptized with the baptism of repentance, saying unto the people, that they should believe on him which should come after him, that is, on Christ Jesus. When they heard this, they were baptized in the name of the Lord Jesus. And when Paul had laid his hands upon them, the Holy Ghost came on them; and they spake with tongues, and prophesied.

In Acts 8, we see a similar occurrence taking place in Samaria. Phillip had preached among the people there and many believed and were baptized.

Now when the apostles which were at Jerusalem heard that Samaria had received the word of God, they sent unto them Peter

*and John: who, when they were come down,
prayed for them, that they might receive the
Holy Ghost: (For as yet he was fallen upon
none of them: only they were baptized in the
name of the Lord Jesus.) Then they laid their
hands on them, and they received the Holy
Ghost.* (verses 14-17 KJV)

Although some denominations today teach that as new believers we automatically receive all of the Holy Spirit that we will ever need at the moment we are born-again, this scripture demonstrates clearly that is not the case. These Samaritans were already born again. They had been baptized in water believing in Jesus' name. Yet they had not received the baptism in the Holy Spirit.

Therefore, we can conclude the baptism in the Holy Spirit is a separate experience from the new birth. It can take place immediately after a person is born again, or it can take place days, months, or even years later. But regardless of when it occurs, this scripture demonstrates, it is a distinctly separate occurrence.

Now, let's look back at the account of the Samaritans and see what happened after they received the baptism in the Holy Spirit.

*When Simon saw that through laying on of
the apostles' hands the Holy Ghost was
given, he offered them money, saying, Give
me also this power, that on whomsoever I
lay hands, he may receive the Holy Ghost.
But Peter said unto him, Thy money perish
with thee, because thou hast thought that
the gift of God may be purchased with
money. Thou hast neither part nor lot in
this matter: for thy heart is not right in the
sight of God.* (verses 18-21 KJV)

Although that passage does not distinctly state that the Samaritans spoke with other tongues, there are two separate indications that they did. The first is found in verse 18 which says, "Simon saw...the Holy Ghost was given." We know that Simon could not possibly have seen the Holy Ghost because He is a Spirit. He is invisible. So Simon must have witnessed an outward demonstration of the Spirit coming upon the Samaritans. In the light of what the book of Acts says about other outpourings of the Holy Spirit, we can safely assume he saw the same evidence the disciples saw in Acts 2, 10 and 19: *speaking in tongues.*

The second indication we have that the Samaritans spoke in tongues can be found in verse 21 where Peter tells Simon he has no part in this matter. The word *matter* there is the Greek word for *utterance*. It is the same word used in Acts 2:4 KJV which says, "They were all filled with the Holy Ghost, and began to speak with other tongues, as the Spirit gave them *utterance*."

Yours for the Asking

All the scriptures we've seen thus far have dealt with groups of believers receiving the baptism of the Holy Spirit. However, when we look at the experience of Saul who eventually became known as the apostle Paul, we see it also can be a very individual experience for it is available any place at any time to any one who asks for it in faith.

Saul was born again through a direct encounter with the Lord Jesus on the road to Damascus. The incident left him blind for three days. At the end of those days, Jesus appeared to a disciple man named Ananias instructing him to go to Saul and minister to him.

> *And Ananias went his way, and entered into the house; and putting his hands on him said, Brother Saul, the Lord, even Jesus, that appeared unto thee in the way as thou camest, hath sent me, that thou mightest*

receive thy sight, and be filled with the Holy Ghost. And immediately there fell from his eyes as it had been scales: and he received sight forthwith, and arose, and was baptized. (Acts 9:17-18 KJV)

Although this particular account does not mention that Saul spoke in tongues, we know he did because he later wrote to the Corinthian church and said, "I thank my God, I speak with tongues more than ye all" (1 Corinthians 14:18 KJV).

In light of all the scriptures we have read, we can draw only one conclusion: *Tongues is a gift given to every believer who receives the baptism in the Holy Spirit.*

If you have not yet had this wonderful experience, I have good news for you. It is yours for the asking. Although it often comes through the laying on of hands, you do not have to wait to receive it until you can find someone to pray for you. Jesus Himself is the One who baptizes us in the Holy Ghost (Mark 1:8) and He said, "If ye then, being evil, know how to give good gifts unto your children: how much more shall your heavenly Father give the Holy Spirit to them that ask him?" (Luke 11:13 KJV).

Why wait another moment? Why not receive this glorious experience now? All you must do is simply ask in faith. Say:

Lord, I come to You in the name of Your Son, Jesus. I have received Him as my Lord and Savior. I have been cleansed of my sins by His precious Blood. Now I have seen in Your Word that the baptism in the Holy Spirit can be mine if I will only ask. So I ask You for it now, Father, and I receive it by faith according to Your Promise. Holy Spirit, rise up within me as I praise God. I fully expect to speak with other tongues as You give me

the utterance. And I thank You for it, in
Jesus' name!

Once you've prayed, begin to speak in heartfelt praise and thanks to God. As you do, syllables you have never before spoken will rise up within you. Speak them out. Don't be nervous about it. Simply relax, lift your heart to God and trust the Holy Spirit. Although you'll have to give voice to the words He gives you (He will not force you to speak), don't concern yourself with how those words sound. Just keep your focus on God. Purpose to express your love and gratitude to Him and enjoy the wonderful gift of tongues!

CHAPTER 14

Understanding the Purposes of Tongues

Wherefore let him that speaketh in an unknown tongue pray that he may inter- pret. For if I pray in an unknown tongue, my spirit prayeth, but my understanding is unfruitful. What is it then? I will pray with the spirit, and I will pray with the under- standing also: I will sing with the spirit, and I will sing with the understanding also.
(1 Corinthians 14:13-15 KJV)

Before we look at the purposes of tongues, it is impor- tant to note that the Bible reveals two different forms of this gift. One is the gift of tongues given to every believer for use in their personal devotional life. The other is the gift of tongues given for public ministry. It is this second form of the gift to which the apostle Paul was referring in 1 Corinthians 14:27-28 KJV when he wrote:

If any man speak in an unknown tongue,
let it be by two, or at the most by three, and
that by course; and let one interpret. But if
there be no interpreter, let him keep silence
in the church; and let him speak to himself,
and to God.

The gift of tongues for public ministry is not available to all believers all the time. It is given to individuals as the Holy Spirit wills. Therefore, in 1 Corinthians 12:29-30 KJV when Paul asked "Are all apostles? are all prophets? are all teachers? are all workers of miracles? Have all the gifts of healing? do all speak with tongues? do all interpret?" the answer is no because Paul was listing tongues as an example of a public ministry gift. He was not referring to the private devotional gift of tongues every Holy Spirit baptized believer enjoys.

With that distinction made, let's turn our attention toward the devotional aspect of tongues to find out exactly how, when and why we should be using it.

An Attitude of Reverence

Speaking in tongues is a vocal miracle. So, no matter how often we do it, we must never cease to reverence it.

We must be careful not to grieve the Holy Spirit by flippantly turning our mouth on *automatic pilot,* chattering away in tongues while our minds wander off to the baseball field or the shopping mall. Such a heartless manifestation of tongues is not only unprofitable for us, it is rude.

We would never treat a treasured friend in such an unthoughtful manner. We wouldn't allow our eyes to roam all around the room when we were talking to her, giving our attention to everything but her presence. So why should we relate to God in such a way?

We shouldn't...yet many times we do. I suppose we have the mistaken idea that because our minds don't understand the words we are saying, it makes no difference what we do with them. Nothing could be further from the truth. For tongues to be the genuine form of communication God designed it to be, we must have our hearts *and minds* hooked up to Him. Mentally we may not be able to grasp exactly what we are saying but we can maintain an attitude of reverence and appreciation for God, turning our attention toward Him as we speak.

Making that one adjustment alone will change the way many of us now use tongues. For if we must employ our whole selves—heart, mind and mouth—in the effort, we won't be so apt to resort to tongues simply because we're too lazy to put together a prayer with our understanding. Forgive me for being blunt, but the plain truth is that's what far too many of us do.

I've seen it over and over again. The pastor will say to the congregation, "Everybody lift your hands and tell Jesus how much you love Him." Immediately half the congregation will start talking in tongues.

The prayer leader will say, "Let's pray for Sister So-and-So." And everybody will automatically start praying in tongues.

Why do we do that? Often it's because we don't want to make the effort to articulate to God what is on our heart.

Tongues were never meant to be used that way. There is something very precious and powerful about speaking to God with our understanding. Using tongues to avoid doing so is an abuse of the gift.

When are we to use tongues then? We are to use them when we are led by the Holy Ghost in order to accomplish a specific, scriptural purpose.

A Wellspring of Worship

The apostle Paul reveals one of those purposes in 1 Corinthians 14:15-17 KJV where he says:

> *...I will pray with the spirit, and I will pray with the understanding also; I will sing with*

*the spirit, and I will sing with the under-
standing also. Else when thou shalt bless
with the spirit, how shall he that occupieth
the room of the unlearned say Amen at thy
giving of thanks, seeing he understandeth
not what thou sayest? For thou verily givest
thanks well, but the other is not edified.*

Tongues can wonderfully enhance and extend your expression of worship to the Lord. When you have praised Him to the limits of your understanding and yet your heart yearns to say more, you can lift your voice and release those sentiments in other tongues.

You can also sing in tongues as you worship the Lord. In fact, Ephesians 5:18-19 KJV specifically instructs us to "be filled with the Spirit; speaking to yourselves in psalms and hymns and spiritual songs, singing and making melody in your heart to the Lord." A spiritual song is a song which comes not from a hymn book or a song sheet, but spontaneously from your spirit. Often as you sing in tongues, you'll find the interpretation of the song rising in your heart and you can sing it out too.

Personally, I've found this kind of worship helps me get into the flow of the Holy Spirit—especially at times when my mind is full of the business of the day and I'm having trouble focusing on the Lord. When I first begin singing in the Spirit, my heart may feel dry and dull. But if I'll release my faith and continue to worship, I'll almost always hit a wellspring of the Spirit. Then, instead of trickling out one drop at a time, songs of praise will flow forth like a river.

Notice I said *if I'll release my faith.* Many Christians don't realize we need to release faith when we pray in tongues but we do. (Remember, we have to use faith with every kind of prayer!)

How can you release your faith if you don't know what you're saying? It's easy. You just believe that as you speak in tongues, the Holy Spirit is accomplishing your intended purpose. For example, if you are worshipping, you believe you are giving thanks well just like the Bible says. By faith, you expect God to inhabit your praises and manifest His presence to you.

"But if I don't know what I am saying, how can I be sure I'm worshipping?" you ask. "How can I be sure I'm not interceding for someone or talking to God about a particular need? After all, the Holy Spirit is there to help me pray about all those things, isn't He?"

Yes, He is—but He wants to work *with you*. He wants to take you in the direction you desire to go.

I often think of praying in tongues like sailboating. When you're in a sailboat you must set your sail to catch the wind so it will take you toward your destination. If you don't set your sail, you won't go anywhere. The wind may be blowing all around you but it won't be doing you any good.

In the same way, the Holy Spirit is always present within you, ready to assist you with the supernatural power to pray in tongues about whatever is on your heart. All you have to do is set your spiritual sail. In my own prayer life, I do that with words. I say, "Holy Spirit, I want to worship the Lord in a deeper way than I can with my understanding right now. So I'm going to worship in tongues for awhile." Then I release my faith and expect Him to help me worship—and He does!

Setting your spiritual sails is a very good habit to adopt because it keeps you from wandering around praying in tongues aimlessly. Effective prayer always has a purpose. *Always.* The purpose may be simply to commune with God through general worship and praise. Or it may be to discuss a specific situation with Him. Either way, prayer must always have purpose or it will not produce results.

When You Don't Know

In addition to enhancing your times of worship, the gift of tongues is invaluable when you are praying about specific people or situations and you're not sure exactly what to pray. Say, for example, your daughter has submitted an application to a particular college she wants to attend and you aren't sure whether that college is a part of God's plan for her life. You can ask God to bring forth His perfect will in the situation, but what can you do if you sense the need to pray further?

Romans 8:26-27 KJV says at times like those:

> *The Spirit...helpeth our infirmities: for we know not what we should pray for as we ought: but the Spirit itself maketh interces-sion for us with groanings which cannot be uttered. And he that searcheth the hearts knoweth what is the mind of the Spirit, because he maketh intercession for the saints according to the will of God.*

In that scripture, the Greek word translated *uttered* refers to articulate speech, or a language we can under-stand. So when you have desires in your heart, you are unable to articulate with natural words, the Holy Spirit comes to your aid and helps you express those desires with spiritual language and at times even with supernatural groanings.

The reason He does so is because we have an *infirm-ity*. Although in modern language we usually use that term in reference to sickness and disease, in the Greek it simply means *an inability to produce results.*

When I was first born again, my inability to produce results in prayer was a source of great struggle and anguish for me. I kept trying to pray but I found I could just go so far and then I'd stop cold because I didn't know what to pray as I ought. When I finally cried out with all my heart, "Lord, help me pray!" He answered by giving me the baptism in the Holy Spirit and the gift of tongues.

From then on, my "infirmity" didn't bother me. When I couldn't produce the results I needed because I didn't know how to pray as I ought, I just prayed in other tongues. Instead of struggling with my inability to produce results, I simply rested in the Holy Spirit's ability. I just depended on my helper, opened my mouth and let Him pray!

After all, He knows far more about the situation than I do. He knows the perfect will of God. So I can release my faith, fully expecting Him to pray the perfect prayer through me.

What causes most of us to continue to struggle in prayer (even though we've been baptized in the Holy Spirit) is not our inability to produce results. On the contrary, it's that we start thinking we are able! So we try in our own strength to pray through to victory. We work to figure things out so we'll know how to pray for them correctly.

I remember once when I slipped into that mindset, I walked around for days thinking and thinking about a certain situation. I looked at it from one angle. Then I looked at it from another. All the time depending on my brain to come up with the solution. Weeks went by and all I had to show for my hours and hours of thinking was a wrinkle in the middle of my forehead.

Finally, I got quiet enough in my heart to hear the voice of the Lord. "*Lynne,*" He said, "*Don't think. Pray!*"

Suddenly, a fresh revelation of my inability to produce results came to me. I stopped struggling and just began to pray in other tongues. Of course, before long I had my answer. The Holy Spirit knew it all the time. He was just waiting for me to look to Him for help.

Tongues for Edification

We can find yet another purpose for tongues in 1 Corinthians 14:4 KJV. There the apostle Paul says, "He that speaketh in an unknown tongue edifieth himself." *Edify* means *to build up, strengthen or fortify.*

Have you ever seen body builders who spend hour upon hour in the gym lifting weights to strengthen their muscles? It's amazing what they can accomplish even though their physical bodies have natural limitations. Our spirits have no such limitations. Just think what we could accomplish if we'd spend more time in the Lord's gym, edifying ourselves by praying in other tongues!

It takes strength to walk with God. It takes spiritual muscle to lay hold of those things for which He has laid hold of us (Philippians 3:12). There are some people who know healing belongs to them. They absolutely know and believe God provided it for them in the atonement. But they are too spiritually weak to receive it. It's sad but it's true.

There are other people who have read in the Bible a thousand times that God loves them and wants to bless them in every way. But they aren't strong enough to apprehend and grasp that love (Ephesians 2:18) so they miss out on His blessings.

What can we do when we detect such weaknesses in ourselves? In addition to feeding on the Word, we can follow the instructions in Jude 20. "But you, beloved, build yourselves up [found] on your most holy faith [make progress, rise like an edifice higher and higher], praying in the Holy Spirit."

Of course you don't have to wait until you feel spiritually weak to edify yourself. You can do it anytime! I find it's especially helpful when I'm wanting to pray but don't seem to have a clear sense of direction. Quite often, after I've prayed in tongues to edify myself for a while, my heart will take hold of something and I'll know which way to go.

There are other times when I just sense the need to enlarge my spiritual capacity so I can rise to a higher level in prayer. At those times, I might determine to pray a set amount of time in other tongues for the purpose of edifying myself. I might do it for 30 minutes as a kind of spiritual exercise.

It's only fair to warn you though, if you've not spent much time praying this way you'll probably be comfortable doing it for only a few minutes at first. Then your flesh will get restless and want to stop. One of the best ways to handle that is to train your spirit like a physical trainer would train an athlete. Set goals and make yourself stretch past your comfort zone. But keep them realistic enough to prevent discouragement.

If you're only comfortable praying in other tongues for 15 minutes, determine to pray for 20 minutes. When 20 minutes becomes comfortable, stretch yourself to 25 or 30 minutes, increasing your capacity a little at a time.

In my own prayer life, I've found that normally after 20 minutes or so of praying in tongues for edification, I'll experience an unction or an anointing. Instead of having to draw out those tongues like water from a well, they'll begin to bubble forth like a spring. That's when it becomes less of a discipline and more of a delight. So I encourage you to set your faith, believe for that unction, and keep praying until it comes.

Praying Mysteries

The fourth and perhaps the most thrilling purpose for praying in tongues is found in 1 Corinthians 14:2 KJV. There, Paul tells us, "He that speaketh in an unknown tongue speaketh not unto men, but unto God: for no man understandeth him: howbeit in the spirit he speaketh mysteries." Here the word *mysteries* actually means *plans and purposes.*

Some time ago, I was at the hospital while a friend of mine was having a baby. As I waited outside the delivery room I thought, *Wouldn't it be nice if every baby came with a handbook that told all about God's plans for his life? Wouldn't it be wonderful if every time he needed guidance or direction, he could just open the handbook and find out which way to go?*

Amazing as it might sound, every one of us actually has such a handbook. God has put it on the inside of us, down in our heart. And the Holy Ghost can search through it, find God's plan for us and then enable us to pray out that plan in other tongues. He can help us pray out our destiny!

Right now you may feel like you're not destined for much of anything, but you are. God planned a course especially for you before you were born. (See Acts 20:22.) But you are not going to stumble onto that course by accident. You must pray about it so you'll be at the right place at the right time. You must speak it forth so God can bring it to pass.

"I don't know how I can possibly do that!" you say. "I have no idea what I'm called to do. The whole thing is a mystery to me."

Then pray out those mysteries! Purpose to reach down into your heart and hook into them. Draw them out reverently and speak them out in tongues to God. Release your faith believing that as you lift those mysteries to Him in prayer, He will answer your prayer by working out His plan in your life.

I know of one particular couple who did that all the way through Bible college. They knew they were called of God to do something. They even sensed it was something big. But they had no idea what it was. So at times, when other students were relaxing or socializing, this couple set themselves to pray in tongues about the destiny God had planned for them. Today they pastor a tremendously successful church, have a nationwide radio ministry and are a blessing to many thousands of people. Because they prayed, they are right on course.

We live in the most critical time in history. This age is rapidly coming to a close. Each of us was born to help bring forth God's grand finale. We cannot afford to roam aimlessly through our lives without knowing and fulfilling our part in it all. So it's absolutely essential for every one of us to spend time praying out these mysteries for our own lives and for the Church as a whole.

Interpreting Your Tongues

What's more, we shouldn't stop there. We shouldn't be content for God's plans to remain mysteries to us. We should go yet a step further, obeying the instructions given us in 1 Corinthians 14:13-14 KJV, "Wherefore let him that speaketh in an unknown tongue pray that he may interpret. For if I pray in an unknown tongue, my spirit prayeth, but my understanding is unfruitful."

God doesn't want to leave you in the dark. He isn't hiding His plans from you. He wants you to understand His plan for your life. He wants you to know His will and the things He has prepared for you. First Corinthians 2 makes that very clear.

> ...*What we are setting forth is a wisdom of God once hidden [from the human understanding] and now revealed to us by God—[that wisdom] which God devised and decreed before the ages for our glorification [to lift us into the glory of His presence]...As the Scripture says, What eye has not seen and ear has not heard and has not entered into the heart of man, [all that] God has prepared (made and keeps ready) for those who love Him...Yet to us God has unveiled and revealed them by and through His Spirit, for the [Holy] Spirit searches diligently, exploring and examining everything, even sounding the profound and bottomless things of God...And we are setting these truths forth in words not taught by human wisdom but taught by the [Holy] Spirit, combining and interpreting spiritual truths with spiritual language [to those who possess the Holy Spirit].* (verses 7, 9, 10, 13)

Did you notice the last sentence? It says we are taught these truths as we interpret spiritual truths with spiritual language. In other words, the mysteries are unveiled as we receive the interpretation of our tongues!

Some people think interpreting their tongues is something so wildly supernatural that as an ordinary Christian they could never do it. Nonsense! The Corinthian church was full of not just ordinary, but downright immature believers. Yet Paul told them to pray that they might interpret their tongues and I don't believe he would have told them to pray for something beyond their spiritual reach.

Actually most people don't have a problem learning to interpret their tongues. They have a problem recognizing the interpretations when they receive them because they often come in such a quiet, unspectacular manner.

Interpretations rarely resound from your lips in King James English the moment you finish praying in tongues. Sometimes, they come hours or even days later. You might spend some time praying in tongues one day, then the next day you might find yourself praying things in English you've never prayed before. You may be speaking truths entirely new to you yet they just flow forth easily because they are coming by the Holy Spirit who is giving you the interpretation of the tongues you prayed the previous day.

At other times, you might be washing dishes or driving down the street when you have a flash of insight. Suddenly you just know something you didn't know before. Perhaps a puzzle piece of God's plan will slip into place and you'll think, *Oh, I see now what God wants me to do in that area of my life!*

What happened? You received the interpretation of those prayers you prayed in tongues.

In my prayer life, I often begin to receive the interpretation of my tongues while I'm actually praying but I usually don't get it all at once. Instead, as I pray in tongues, English words or phrases will come to me. They may not make any sense to me at first, but I'll speak them out in faith anyway, expecting God to further my understanding.

I don't sit there and try to put together an interpretation with those words. I just keep praying in tongues and waiting on God until a revealing comes to my spirit. Sometimes even after I receive that revealing, I may not be able to articulate it. So I just keep praying in tongues and often a few days later, the articulation will come and I'll be able to speak the mystery out clearly in English.

Right now, you may be thinking you could never do this. But, believe me, you can! We have little children at our church who can interpret their tongues. What's their secret? They simply believe.

As with every other aspect of prayer, your ability to interpret your tongues will increase as you develop your faith and continue to practice. You'll probably start by taking one small step at a time. You may get just a word of interpretation here and a word there.

When you do, just thank God for it. Ask Him to enable you to go further and then expect the Holy Ghost to help you as you continue to explore the glorious mysteries of God.

CHAPTER 15

The Realms of the Spirit

But as it is written, Eye hath not seen, nor ear heard, neither have entered into the heart of man the things which God hath prepared for them that love him. But God hath revealed them unto us by his Spirit.
(1 Corinthians 2:9-10 KJV)

Once you start learning to cooperate with the Holy Spirit, you will discover that prayer is a more magnificent occupation than you ever imagined. You will find it is not just the Holy Spirit helping you pray about the matters that concern you. It is you helping the Holy Spirit pray about the matters that concern Him.

The very concept staggers the imagination. If it were not in the Bible, it would be impossible to believe almighty God could possibly desire the aid and assistance of the likes of us—reborn creations though we are. Yet from cover to cover, the Word of God reveals that since the beginning when God gave man dominion over the earth, He has worked in partnership with men and women of faith and prayer.

Over and over in the pages of scripture we hear Him say, "Ask! Ask of Me!" Behind those fervent admonitions is the loving heart of a Father who longs to pour out blessings upon the earth. Yet He restrains Himself. He has given the earth to mankind and He will not usurp our authority. He waits to be invited.

Throughout the Old Testament He always found a remnant who would do so; God-loving people who yielded themselves as servants and, under the power of the Holy Spirit, prayed God's will into the earth. But now He has something much greater. He has millions of born-again men and women who are not just servants but *sons* with His own nature and His own Spirit living in their hearts.

Not Just Spectators—Participators!

My, how we have underestimated the call God has given us! The apostle Paul gives us a glimpse of it in 1 Corinthians 1:9 when he says, "God is faithful (reliable, trustworthy, and therefore ever true to His promise, and He can be depended on); by Him you were called into companionship and participation with His Son, Jesus Christ our Lord."

We are not called to be forever spiritual infants constantly crying for our Father to do this and that for us. We are called to grow up and become participators and companions with Him, helping Him fulfill His purposes and intents for all eternity. That is what prayer is truly all about.

"Well, I can easily see how I need God but I just don't see how *God* could need *me!*"

Can't you? Think about it for a moment. The Bible says the Holy Spirit is an intercessor. But how does He get that work of intercession done? Romans 8:26 tells us. He "goes to meet *our* supplication!" He cannot pray unless we pray. He is dependent on us just as we are dependent on Him. And even as we have things in our lives we want to pray about, He has things He wants to pray about—whole realms of them!

The realms of the Holy Spirit are incredibly vast. They include not only this physical universe and all that is in it— from the leaders of nations to the baby bird in its nest; they also include dimensions of the Spirit no man has ever seen. They extend beyond the here and now, backward through the ages of time, and forward through the eons of eternity.

Although it's difficult to imagine what the Holy Spirit does with all those realms, the first chapter of Genesis gives us some insight. It says that in the beginning when the earth was without form and darkness was on the face of the deep, "the Spirit of God moved upon the face of the waters" (verse 2 KJV). The word moved actually means to hover like a mother hen hovers over her eggs.

The Holy Spirit's desire as He hovered over this earth was to release His power and bring forth life according to the will of God. But He did not do so until God spoke. He did not split the darkness until He heard the Words, "Let there be light" (verse 3).

Today the Holy Spirit is still hovering over the realms of God. And today, just as in the beginning, He is waiting for someone to speak God's words and will over those realms. He is waiting for us to ask in the name of Jesus. He is waiting for us to yield ourselves to Him in prayer and say, "Let there be light in the life of that lost soul! Let there be life for the dying one! Let God's will be done on earth as it is in heaven!"

But, for the most part, we have not done it. It's not necessarily because we've been unwilling, it's because we haven't known about those realms—much less expected the Holy Spirit to reveal them to us. We've puttered around praying from our limited earthly perspective, totally unaware that if we would but release our faith, the Spirit of grace and supplication within us would open to us the eternal universe of God Himself.

Realms Revealed

The simple fact is, we cannot participate with God in a realm unless He reveals it to us—but once He does, it is easy. I am living proof of that. There was a time in my life when I had no heartfelt burden to pray for the lost. I knew I should have, but I didn't.

Of course, I was glad whenever someone was born again. I would say, "Oh good. Praise the Lord!" But then I went on with my happy life. I didn't think much about the people in my city who were lost. I didn't feel deeply on their behalf because I had no real revelation of that realm.

Then one day I was reading a book about a man named David Brainerd who cared so much for the lost Indians of his day, he would pray in the snow for hours in anguish for their souls. When I saw that I said, "Lord, I confess I don't have that kind of burden for the lost but I want to have it. So I'm asking You for it now."

Sometimes I think I should never have made that request. Since then there have been times when the Holy Spirit opened that realm of lost humanity and made it so real to my heart that I could feel what it's like to be slipping toward hell with no one to help. I have seen the utter darkness. I have heard the heartrending cries.

At times when I begin to lose the awareness of that realm, the Holy Spirit gives me visions and dreams to rekindle it. He does whatever I need Him to do to keep the revelation fresh so I will pray.

Of course, it's easy to see how important the realm of lost humanity would be to the Holy Spirit. But when you begin to yield to Him and let Him take you into His realms, you'll find there are other things He is concerned about too. One day as you're praying, He might begin to show you the outpouring of God's glory that is coming on the Church. And you'll rejoice and say, "My, the glory is a big, important realm!"

Then He might wake you up in the night and show you a mother dog and her puppies about to freeze in a barn somewhere. So you stay up watching and praying over those puppies all night.

You may think praying for puppies is silly and certainly not as important as praying for God's glory in the Church. But if puppies are what the Holy Spirit is leading you to pray for, then those puppies are very important. You see, every realm is precious in the sight of God. As the Bible says, not one sparrow falls to the ground without His notice (Matthew 10:29).

What's more, the Holy Spirit understands and knows all the future of each realm. He may know, for example, that one of those puppies will one day save a child's life. Will He tell you that when He leads you to pray for them? Not necessarily. So we must simply trust Him and pray as He directs.

Praying by the Spirit of Prophecy

"Well, Sister Hammond, that sounds exciting. I just believe the next time I pray, I'll try to get into one of those realms."

No, don't make that mistake. You never get into these places by trying. If you start trying to do it, you'll be vulnerable to deception. What you need to do is just keep your eyes on Jesus. Make sure your purpose is simply to know and obey Him. Keep building your faith by meditating the Word and fellowshipping with the Lord. Then, follow the promptings of the Holy Spirit whenever they come.

Also, be patient. You don't step into these places overnight. It takes time. You may notice when you first begin, you can only pick up a word or two in your spirit. If so, just lift up those words to the Lord.

You see, this kind of prayer comes by the spirit of prophecy. Contrary to what many people think, prophecy isn't just standing up in church declaring future events. Prophecy is utterance inspired by the Holy Spirit. It is the voice of God speaking through you bringing exhortation, edification or comfort (1 Corinthians 14:3), and it doesn't always manifest the same way .

Sometimes when the spirit of prayer comes upon you, you will pray in other tongues. At other times you'll speak with your understanding. There will even be times when it will cause you to groan or weep. But whatever form it takes, the spirit of prophecy is the voice of God speaking through you in prayer.

Oh, how desperately we need His voice speaking through our prayers in these days! For when He speaks, things are changed, conditions in spiritual realms are altered, making way for the move of God in the hearts of men. As Isaiah 40:3-5 says, that prophectic voice is—

A voice of one who cries: Prepare in the wilderness the way of the Lord [clear away the obstacles]; make straight and smooth in the desert a highway for our God! Every valley shall be lifted and filled up, and every mountain and hill shall be made low; and the crooked and uneven shall be made straight and level, and the rough places a plain. And the glory (majesty and splendor) of the Lord shall be revealed, and all flesh shall see it together; for the mouth of the Lord has spoken it.

In Isaiah's day, when a king would travel to a new place, a group of people would go before and clear a path for him. They would make ready the roads, filling in the ruts and leveling out the bumps so the king's ride would be smooth and easy.

In the same way, God sends praying people before His coming to make a way for Him. The tools He gives us to use are His Words. Think of it! By speaking the inspired Words of God by the anointing of the Holy Spirit, we clear a highway for our God! We clear a path in the realms of the spirit so He can move and work.

We haven't seen much of this spirit of prayer in the Church in recent times. But we can read about it in years past and see just what marvelous things can happen when it is present in the lives of God's people. During the 1800's, the great evangelist, Charles Finney spoke of one man in particular upon whom rested this wonderful spirit of prayer.

His name was Mr. Abel Clary and, although licensed to preach, he spent the greatest part of his life and ministry in prayer. At times, he would come to the cities in which Brother Finney was preaching. His burden of prayer would often be so great that instead of attending the meetings, he would stay in his room and pray.

In writing of him, Charles Finney records one particular time when he was having dinner with Mr. Clary and his brother. Mr. Clary bowed his head in prayer intending only to speak a blessing over the food. Suddenly, he broke down and fled to his room. Brother Finney followed him there and found him seemingly in great distress.

> "He lay groaning upon the bed, the spirit making intercession for him, and in him, with groanings that could not be uttered. I had barely entered the room, when he made out to say, 'Pray, Brother Finney.' I knelt down and helped him in prayer, by leading his soul out for the conversion of sinners...I understood that this was the voice of God. I saw the Spirit of prayer was upon him, and I felt His influence upon myself, and took it for granted that the work would move on powerfully." (How to Pray, R.A. Torrey, Whitaker House, 1983, p. 99-100)

Brother Finney's work in that city did indeed move on powerfully. During the six weeks he was there, 500 people were saved.

Be Willing to Grow

We must ask the Lord for such a spirit of prayer in our lives today! But we must not demand to start at the level achieved by seasoned saints like Mr. Abel Clary. We must humble ourselves and be willing to start where all beginners do—at the beginning—and be willing to grow in this gift that only God can give.

Have you ever noticed that when someone who has recently been born again stands up in church to prophecy, their message is usually very simple and basic? They may even stumble and make some mistakes. The first time I prophesied in a public service I said, "The Lord would say to you this morning..."The problem was, it wasn't morning—it was evening. Of course, God knew what time it was. But I was just starting out and learning to flow in prophecy. I hadn't developed in it very far yet.

Romans 12:6 says, "Having gifts...that differ according to the grace given us, let us use them: [He whose gift is] prophecy, [let him prophesy] according to the proportion of his faith."When it comes to prophecy—whether in public ministry or in your private prayer time—the more you develop your faith through the Word and through practice, the more easily and accurately you will be able to flow in that gift. Practice!

Exploring the Bottomless Things of God

Since the gifts are a result of God's grace at work in you, you can accelerate your development by asking Him to increase your capacity in prayer. He'll do it. He wants to take us higher. He wants to take us on marvelous adventures in prayer and show us the great plans and realms of God. That's not just what I say. That's what the Bible says!

> *...As the Scripture says, What eye has not seen and ear has not heard and has not entered into the heart of man, [all that] God has prepared (made and keeps ready) for those who love Him [who hold Him in affectionate reverence, promptly obeying Him and gratefully recognizing the benefits He has bestowed. Yet to us God has unveiled and revealed them by*

*and through his Spirit, for the [Holy] Spirit
searches diligently, exploring and examining
everything, even sounding the profound and
bottomless things of God [the divine counsels
and things hidden and beyond man's scruti-
ny].* (1 Corinthians 2:9-10)

There are wondrous things that physical eyes have
never seen and physical ears have never heard. There are
realms so vast no human being could ever even think of
them. Yet God has revealed them to us by His Spirit!

If you'll learn to yield to Him in faith, the Holy Spirit
will lead you to pray things that will absolutely astonish you.
You'll hear yourself praying out truths and revelations and
you'll think, "How in the world did I ever come up with that?
I never thought of it before in my life!"

I'll tell you how you came up with it. It was on the
inside of you, in your heart. All the deep and bottomless
things of God are in there because that's where the Holy
Spirit dwells—and those realms are all in Him.

Just imagine! Every answer you'll ever need to know,
the whole of God's divine counsel, all His plans for the
future—*everything!*—is inside you right now. And the
Holy Spirit is desiring to reveal those realms to you. Why?
So you can become a participator in them! So you can
work with Him through prayer and bring God's will to pass
in those realms!

A Look at the Master

To see just how supernatural those kinds of prayers
can be, all we have to do is look at the Master of prayer, Jesus
Himself. The prayer He prayed just before He went to the
cross is the most remarkable ever recorded and it is a wonderful demonstration of praying by the Holy Ghost.

When He prayed it, He was about to face the most hor-
rible experience any man had ever known. He was about to

be betrayed. He was about to die a painful death. And worst
of all, He was about to bear the sin of the whole human race
and, in so doing, be separated from His heavenly Father.

Yet, as we read the prayer recorded in John 17, we find
He made mention of none of these things. That is because
He was not praying from the present, earthly realm. He was
praying by the spirit of prophecy about higher realms than
that. He said:

> *Father, the hour is come; glorify thy Son, that
> thy Son also may glorify thee: as thou hast
> given him power over all flesh, that he
> should give eternal life to as many as thou
> hast given him. And this is life eternal, that
> they might know thee the only true God,
> and Jesus Christ, whom thou hast sent. I
> have glorified thee on the earth: I have
> finished the work which thou gavest me
> to do. And now, O Father, glorify thou me
> with thine own self with the glory which I
> had with thee before the world was.*
> (verses 1-5 KJV)

This is very interesting when you think about it. The
greatest work God had given Jesus to do was to bear the sin
of mankind on the cross. Naturally speaking, He had not yet
done that. But He said, "I have finished the work" because He
was not praying in the realm of the present. He was praying
about the glorification that was to be His on the other side
of the cross, several days hence.

Why was He praying about that? Because that was
what the Holy Spirit was showing Him. That was the realm
He was seeing and hearing about in His heart.

> *I have manifested thy name unto the men
> which thou gavest me out of the world: thine
> they were, and thou gavest them me...For I*

*have given unto them the words which thou
gavest me; and they have received them, and
have known surely that I came out from
thee, and they have believed that thou didst
send me. I pray for them: I pray not for the
world but for them which thou hast given
me; for they are thine. And all mine are
thine, and thine are mine; and I am glorified in them. And now I am no more in the
world, but these are in the world, and I
come to thee. Holy Father, keep through
thine own name those whom thou hast
given me, that they may be one, as we are.*
(verses 6, 8-11 KJV)

Here Jesus begins to pray from the future realm of
His High Priestly Ministry about a time when He will be
glorified—or fully made known—in His disciples. He con-
tinues praying:

*While I was with them in the world, I kept
them in thy name: those that thou gavest me
I have kept, and none of them is lost, but the
son of perdition; that the scripture might be
fulfilled...As thou hast sent me into the
world, even so have I sent them into the
world.* (verse 12, 18 KJV)

Now to you and me, Jesus' statements make perfect
sense because we know Judas was about to betray Him. We
know that approximately 40 days after this He would issue
the Great Commission and tell the disciples to go into all the
world and preach. But keep in mind, none of those things
had happened yet. So the disciples who were listening to
this prayer must have been thinking, *What?! What is He talking about? Who is the son of perdition? What is this about
being sent? He hasn't sent us anywhere!*

Sometimes, as you pray by the unction of the Holy Spirit, you'll feel just like those disciples. You'll hear yourself pray things from your heart and your mind will say, "*What on earth does that mean? That's the strangest thing I've ever heard in my life!*" That's because you're seeing things to come and you don't yet fully understand them.

To Our Day...and Beyond

Now let's move forward in Jesus' prayer to verse 20 where He says:

> *Neither pray I for these alone, but for them*
> *also which shall believe on me through their*
> *word; that they all may be one; as thou,*
> *Father, art in me, and I in thee, that they*
> *also may be one in us: that the world may*
> *believe that thou hast sent me. And the glory*
> *which thou gavest me I have given them;*
> *that they may be one even as we are one. I*
> *in them, and thou in me, that they may be*
> *made perfect in one; and that the world*
> *may know that thou hast sent me, and hast*
> *loved them, as thou hast loved me.*
> (verses 20-23 KJV)

At this point Jesus steps into the realm which contains everyone who would ever believe. That realm includes you and me—and it extends at least 2,000 years beyond the moment in time when Jesus prayed this prayer! You might think it would be enough to pray 2,000 years into the future, but He doesn't stop there. He prays further about a time in which all Christians will be one and so full of the glory of God the whole world will know Jesus is the Messiah!

To look at the Church right now, you might think that could never happen. But Jesus prayed it, and if He prayed it, we know He saw it in the Holy Spirit. So we can be sure that one way or another, it is going to come to pass.

Finally, Jesus concludes His prayer by spanning the spiritual universe—from before the foundation of the world all the way to the rapture. He says, "Father, I will that they also, whom thou hast given me, be with me where I am; that they may behold my glory, which thou hast given me: for thou lovedst me before the foundation of the world."

Isn't it thrilling to watch the Master pray? Isn't it marvelous to see how effortlessly He moves throughout the realms of God, speaking forth those things God has declared and planned from ages past for the eons to come?

Let us learn from His example. Let us follow Him, leave earth's limited perspective behind and let the same Holy Spirit who led Him, lead us into those supernatural places. Let us fall on our knees in faith and cry, "Lord, help us pray!"

CHAPTER 16

The Power of Perserverance

Do not, therefore, fling away your fearless confidence, for it carries a great and glorious compensation of reward. For you have need of steadfast patience and endurance, so that you may perform and fully accomplish the will of God, and thus receive and carry away [and enjoy to the full] what is promised. (Hebrews 10:35-36)

It is thrilling and rewarding to pray by the unction of the Holy Spirit and explore with Him the realms of God. But for those prayers to produce the results you desire, there is another element that must be added. It is the element of perseverance.

To persevere means *to see something all the way through to the end.* It means once God puts a person or a situation in your heart, you stay with it. You keep praying...and praying...and praying God's will in that matter until you see that prayer fully answered, or until the burden lifts and you sense in your spirit the victory has been won. At times it may seem every demon in hell is trying to shake your confidence. It may appear that the more you pray, the worse the situation becomes. But, even so, you refuse to give up until God's will is done.

Sound like hard work? It is. The apostle Paul likens it to a military battle and says you must be spiritually armed and strong to do it.

> *Finally, my brethren, be strong in the Lord, and in the power of his might. Put on the whole armour of God, that ye may be able to stand against the wiles of the devil. For we wrestle not against flesh and blood, but against principalities, against powers, against the rulers of the darkness of this world, against spiritual wickedness in high places. Wherefore take unto you the whole armour of God, that ye may be able to withstand in the evil day, and having done all, to stand. Stand therefore, having your loins girt about with truth, and having on the breastplate of righteousness; and your feet shod with the preparation of the gospel of peace; above all, taking the shield of faith, wherewith ye shall be able to quench all the fiery darts of the wicked. And take the helmet of salvation, and the sword of the Spirit which is the word of God: **praying always with all prayer and supplication in the Spirit, and watching thereunto with all perseverance and supplication for all saints**. (Ephesians 6:10-18 KJV)*

Many years ago, I saw how very powerful perseverance can be through the life of a precious Christian named Bill. He attended the denominational church where I was teaching a Sunday school class of four and five year-olds. Every Sunday, Bill gathered up the neighborhood children, loaded them into his station wagon and brought them to church with him.

One of those children was in my class and he was the most uncontrollable child I've ever seen. He would crawl under the table while I was telling Bible stories and bite my leg. He would climb the bookshelves like a monkey. He was a constant disruption. Although his condition had a medical name, considering the fact that both of his parents were not only unsaved but also alcoholics, I realize now he was probably demon possessed.

One day one of the deacons of the church walked in and saw him in the midst of one of his fits. When the deacon found out he acted that way every week, he met with the other deacons about the situation and they decided the little boy could not be allowed to come back to church.

I'll never forget the look on Bill's face when they told him. He looked at them like they were the most wicked men he'd ever seen. "All right," he said, "if you will let this child continue to come to Sunday School, I promise to stay with him the whole time and make sure he does not disrupt." The deacons agreed and for years afterward, Bill loved and tended to that child faithfully every Sunday.

Since Mac and I moved away from that town many years ago, I never knew what happened to that little boy. So once when I went back to visit, I asked a friend about him. "Oh, it's the most wonderful thing!" she said. "That little boy graduated from high school and now he is in Bible college. He wants to be a preacher!"

Many times when I'm tempted to give up on someone in prayer, I think about Bill. I think of what would have happened to that little boy if he hadn't persevered. And I'm encouraged to keep praying.

Faith in Action

"But wait," you may say, "I thought praying in faith meant you pray once, believe you receive and never pray about that particular matter again!"

In some instances, that is true. When it comes to obtaining things for yourself that are yours by virtue of redemption, all you have to do is reach out in faith and receive them. If you need healing, for instance, there's no reason to travail and labor over it in prayer. The Bible says that by the stripes of Jesus you *were* healed. Healing is already yours. So all you need to do is believe the Word, pray the prayer of faith and then say, "Thank you, Lord. From this moment forward, I consider myself healed! Amen."

When it comes to praying for other people, however, there is often a need to continue in prayer over a period of time. Such perseverance is not an indication of unbelief. On the contrary, according to the Bible, it is faith in action. It is proof that the person praying is so certain God will answer their prayer, they keep on pressing through until that answer comes.

Elijah had that kind of persistence in prayer. Let's read again what James said about him.

> *The earnest (heartfelt, continued) prayer of a righteous man makes tremendous power available [dynamic in its working]. Elijah was a human being with a nature such as we have...and he prayed earnestly for it not to rain, and no rain fell on the earth for three years and six months. And [then he prayed again and the heavens supplied rain and the land produced its crops [as usual].* (James 5:16b-18)

If you'll read the story recorded in 1 Kings 18 recounting the time when Elijah's prayer brought back the rain, you'll find Elijah didn't just pray once, believe and forget it. He went up on Mount Carmel, knelt down on the ground with his face between his knees and prayed until he saw the manifestation of what God had put in his heart. It didn't come instantly, either.

And [Elijah] said to his servant, Go up now,
look toward the sea. And he went up, and
looked, and said, There is nothing. And he
said, Go again seven times. And it came to
pass at the seventh time, that he said,
Behold, there ariseth a little cloud out of the
sea, like a man's hand. And he said, Go up,
say unto Ahab, Prepare thy chariot, and get
thee down, that the rain stop thee not. And it
came to pass in the mean while, that the
heaven was black with clouds and wind,
and there was a great rain.
(verses 43-45 KJV)

Can't you just imagine that poor servant huffing and puffing, running to his lookout point and then back to Elijah?

"I don't see any clouds, Sir."

"Well, then go look again while I keep praying."

"Still, nothing there, Sir."

"Then go again, while I keep praying."

"But, Sir, I've been six times already!"

"What difference does that make, son? We know the rain is coming. God said it is. So get up there and watch for it while I keep praying!"

Don't Settle for Less Than 100%

Some things you pray about won't require such persistence. But others will. Back in 1979, for instance, the Lord started revealing to me the glory He desires to pour out upon the Church. He put the vision of it in my heart so I could pray for it. Do you know what? I'm *still* praying for the glory today. Although we're seeing more miracles and experiencing more glorious outpourings of the Spirit than we have in years past, the full glory I have seen in my heart hasn't yet manifested. So I intend to persist in prayer until it does.

As people of prayer we shouldn't be willing to settle for 50 percent victory. We shouldn't be willing to settle for 75 percent victory. We should not even be willing to settle for 99 percent victory. We must determine to pray until we get 100 percent victory—because our God is mighty enough to give it to us!

What's more, He is looking for people with that kind of persistence in prayer these days. We're coming to the end of the age. The powers of darkness are running rampant because the Devil knows he has little time left. Many Christians are throwing up their hands and saying, "Not much can be done now! Let's just try to hang on till Jesus comes!" But the Lord is searching through the body of Christ to find people with a different kind of attitude who will become soldiers in His army of prayer.

He is looking for people who will commit to pray faithfully; people who will say, "You can depend on me, Lord. I'll take whatever assignment You give me and pray it all the way through to victory. I know I can do it because greater is He that is in me than He that is in the world!"

Now more than ever, God is needing people like the widow Jesus described in Luke 18 who prayed without fainting and refused to turn coward, lose heart or give up. That widow didn't have a loving, heavenly Father to turn to like we do when we pray. She was dealing with a wicked judge who neither feared God nor respected man. Yet she kept coming to him and saying:

> *Avenge me of mine adversary. And he would not for a while: but afterward he said within himself, Though I fear not God, nor regard man; yet because this widow troubleth me, I will avenge her, lest by her continual coming she weary me. And the Lord said, Hear what the unjust judge saith. And shall not God avenge his own elect, which*

*cry day and night unto him, though he bear
long with them? I tell you that he will
avenge them speedily. Nevertheless when the
Son of man cometh, shall he find faith on
the earth?* (verses 3-8)

In that last statement, Jesus reminds us that when we persevere in prayer we must do it in faith. Speaking the same words day after day in an empty ritualistic manner is nothing more than vain repetition and it is useless. True persevering prayer isn't like that. It is as heartfelt the fiftieth time as it was the first time it was prayed and it's always accompanied by a childlike confidence that expects God to do what He promised—no matter how long it takes.

That means when you pray perseveringly, you don't get up off your knees, look at the situation and say, "Oh my, it doesn't look like my prayer did any good. I guess I'd better pray again."

No, every time you pray you must believe your prayers changed things in the realm of the spirit even if you cannot yet see evidence of those changes in the natural world. You must believe God heard you and went to work on your behalf. But you must also understand there are forces of darkness working to hinder the answer to your prayer, and so you must be willing to stick with the process until you've prayed the answer all the way through.

Plead Your Case

There is only one thing that will give you that kind of tenacity: *the Word of God.*

To keep praying in faith in spite of all the adverse circumstances and negative reports that often come along, you must not only know what the Bible promises you, you must see a clear inner image of that promise being fulfilled. It must shine within you so brightly it chases away every shadow of doubt.

Sometimes people will tell me about a situation and say, "Well, you know, Sister Hammond, I'm just praying and standing on the Word."

"Really?" I'll say. "Exactly what scriptures in the Word are you standing on?"

You'd be amazed how many times they can't tell me. They just shrug as if to say, "The whole Bible, I guess."

Listen, you can't base your prayer request on a general belief in the Bible. You have to be specific. You have to study the Scriptures and find out exactly what you can expect God to do in your particular situation.

In some ways, praying is like presenting a legal case. And in the courtroom of heaven, the only acceptable law is the Word of God. Now, even though the Judge is your heavenly Father and He desires to rule in your favor, He can only do so if you base your case on promises and precedent from the Bible.

That's why in Isaiah 43:25-26 KJV, He says, "I, even I, am he that blotteth out thy transgression for mine own sake, and will not remember thy sins. Put me in remembrance: let us plead together: declare thou, that thou mayest be justified."

When God says *Put Me in remembrance,* He's not telling you to remind Him of what a great person you are or how very much you want your prayer answered. He is telling you to put Him in remembrance of His Word. For according to divine law, that Word is the only plea to which He can respond.

As Isaiah 62:6-7 says:

*I have set watchmen upon your walls, O
Jerusalem, who will never hold their peace
day or night; you who [are His servants and
by your prayers] put the Lord in remembrance [of His promises], keep not silence,
and give Him no rest until He establishes
Jerusalem and makes her a praise in
the earth.*

Your job in prayer is to hold God's Word before Him and keep it there until that Word is manifested in the person or situation for which you are praying. You are to put together an airtight case based on the specific scriptures and to keep pleading that case in the court of heaven until your adversary, the Devil, gives up and goes home.

Of course, you don't have to do it by yourself. You have the Holy Spirit to help you. One of His names is *Advocate*. An advocate is a lawyer who pleads another's case.

As your Advocate, the Holy Spirit will lead you to the scriptures you need. He'll quicken them to your heart. He'll help you bring forth your case with such eloquence (both in other tongues and with your understanding) that the Devil won't stand a chance against you. Then He'll help you stand strong until your case is fully won.

Get Yourself Stirred Up!

Sadly enough, even though that kind of power in prayer is readily available to every believer, we see little of it among us. Isaiah 64:7 KJV tells us the reason. "There is none that calleth upon thy name, that stirreth up himself to take hold of thee."

Too many times we sit around waiting for someone else to get us stirred up enough to take hold of God's Word. We can't afford to do that. We must get *ourselves* stirred up—and we must do it now!

If you want to see just how great an impact you can have by taking hold of God's Word and lifting it before Him in prayer, consider Daniel. His people, the Jews, had been living as captives in the nation of Babylon for more than 70 years. At that time it must have looked like they would be captives there forever. But one day as Daniel was reading the Scriptures, something caught his attention. In Daniel 9:2-3, he writes:

> *I, Daniel, understood by the books the num-*
> *ber of years which, according to the word of*

*the Lord to Jeremiah the prophet, must pass
by before the desolations [which had been]
pronounced on Jerusalem should end; and it
was seventy years. And I set my face to the
Lord to seek Him by prayer and supplica-
tions and sackcloth and ashes.*

Daniel saw in the book of Jeremiah that God had
promised to deliver the Jews from captivity after 70 years!
So what did he do? Did he sit around crying about the miserable situation of his nation? Did he sit around wondering
why God hadn't already set them free?

No! He took hold of God's promise and began to pray
for the fulfillment of it. He *set his face* to seek the Lord about
the matter. In other words, he determined in his heart not to
give up on this prayer until it was answered.

As a result of Daniel's prayers, the book of Ezra tells us
that God stirred the heart of a wicked king named Cyrus. As
a result, he not only released the Jews from Babylon, he sent
them back to rebuild the temple at Jerusalem and provided
the finances they needed to get the job done! Keep in mind
now, Cyrus wasn't a man of God. He wasn't even a very nice
person. But God moved on him anyway.

Why? Because Daniel prayed. He didn't wait for anyone else to inspire him. He didn't wait for natural conditions
to improve. He stirred himself up to take hold of God, believing that if he prayed, God would fulfill His Word.

It's also interesting to note that the Jews themselves
weren't behaving in a particularly godly fashion at that time.
Daniel said they had done wickedly, forsaking the law of
God and refusing to heed the words of the prophets. They
didn't even deserve to be set free. But Daniel didn't base his
prayer upon their righteousness. He based it upon the Word
of God and His great mercy and loving kindness. (See Daniel
9:18.)

I wonder how many Christians are living in bondage
today, how many sinners are about to slip into hell, how
many nations are in captivity because God could find no one

like Daniel to pray His mercy down upon them? How many times have we as believers stood by self-righteously shaking our heads over the plight of some wicked group of people thinking they simply got what they had coming, when all the while our tender, merciful God was saying:

> *I sought a man among them who should*
> *build up the wall and stand in the gap*
> *before Me for the land, that I should not*
> *destroy it, but I found none. Therefore have*
> *I poured out My indignation upon them,*
> *I have consumed them with the fire of My*
> *wrath: their own way have I repaid [by*
> *bringing] it upon their own heads, says the*
> *Lord God.* (Ezekiel 22:30-31)

It Only Takes One

One of the most important things we as praying people must remember in every situation is that God does not want to send judgment on people. He delights in mercy. So, He is always looking for a way to preserve people and deliver them from their sin and its consequences.

The first thing God does when He sees that judgment is about to strike, is search for a man or woman who will stop that judgment by standing between it and the person who is about to be judged. He looks for someone who will ask Him for mercy. He doesn't search for a multitude of people, or even a small crowd of people. *All He needs is one person who will pray.*

That's why in Genesis 18, God went to tell Abraham, His Friend, of the impending destruction of Sodom and Gomorrah. He wanted Abraham to use his covenant relationship with God to ask for mercy for those cities. And that is exactly what Abraham did. He stood before the Lord and said:

Will you destroy the righteous...together with
the wicked? Suppose there are in the city fifty
righteous; will You destroy the place and not
spare it (for the sake of) the fifty righteous
in it? Far be it from You to do such a thing,
to slay the righteous with the wicked, so that
the righteous fare as do the wicked! be that
far from You! Shall not the Judge of all the
earth execute judgment and do righteously.
(verses 23-25)

Notice, Abraham didn't stand on the side of wrath. He
didn't say, "Yes, Lord. Those are terrible cities. I think You
should just burn them to the ground. "Abraham stood on the
side of the people of Sodom and Gomorrah and cried out in
their behalf.

What was God's response? Did He say, "Forget it,
Abraham. I'm going to wipe out those people and you can't
stop Me." No, He said, "If I find in the city of Sodom fifty righteous...I will spare the whole place for their sakes."

God listened to Abraham. He granted his requests for
mercy—not just one time but five different times. When
Abraham said, "Will you spare the city for the sake of 45
righteous?" God said, "Yes."

When Abraham said, "Will you spare it for the sake of
40...or 30...or 20...or 10?" Each time, God answered, "Yes."

The people of Sodom didn't deserve mercy. They
weren't on their knees asking God for forgiveness, but
Abraham was asking in their behalf. That's what intercessory
prayer is. It is standing in the gap, asking God to give someone else something for which they're not even asking. It is
asking Him to give them more mercy than they deserve.

"But wait a minute," you may say, "the city of Sodom
was destroyed!"

Yes, but not because God refused to save it. He
granted every request Abraham made on behalf of that city.
When God agreed to save it for the sake of 10 righteous peo-

ple, Abraham stopped asking. The problem was, there were not 10 righteous people living there.

What would have happened if Abraham had asked God for even more mercy? What would have happened if he simply had said, "Lord, will you save this city for my sake alone?"

I believe Abraham had such leverage and such a strong covenant relationship with God, that God's answer would have been *yes.*

The reason I believe so is because God did that very thing in Exodus 32. There, the Bible tells us the children of Israel forsook God and made a golden calf to worship just days after He had brought them miraculously out of Egypt. Their sin was so great it provoked God to judgment and He said to Moses who had been with Him on Mount Sinai:

> *...Go down; for your people, whom you have brought out of the land of Egypt, have corrupted themselves. They have turned aside quickly out of the way which I commanded them; they have made them a molten calf, and have worshipped it and sacrificed to it, and said, These are your gods, O Israel, that brought you up out of Egypt! And the Lord said to Moses, I have seen this people, and behold, it is a stiffnecked people; Now therefore let Me alone, that My wrath may burn hot against them, and that I may destroy them; but I will make of you a great nation.* (verses 7-10)

God's Word in Man's Mouth

Did you notice what God said there? He said, "Let me alone." Judgment comes on people when we let God alone.

Many people say, "Well, God is God and He is going to have His way." No! He won't have His way unless we pray.

You see, even though God has judgment, He is love.

Love is His nature. Love is His way. That's why the Bible says, mercy triumphs over judgment (James 2:13). Mercy is God's higher law.

If Moses had let God alone concerning the people of Israel, they would have been destroyed. Moses could have said, "Great! Go for it, God! Just let them burn and You and I will start all over again." But he didn't. Instead, He invoked the higher law of mercy and said:

> *...Lord, why does Your wrath blaze hot*
> *against Your people, whom You have*
> *brought forth out of the land of Egypt with*
> *great power and a mighty hand? Why*
> *should the Egyptians say, For evil He*
> *brought them forth, to slay them in the*
> *mountains and consume them from the face*
> *of the earth? Turn from Your fierce wrath,*
> *and change Your mind concerning this evil*
> *against Your people. [Earnestly] remember*
> *Abraham, Isaac, and Israel, Your servants, to*
> *whom You swore by Your own self and said*
> *to them, I will multiply your seed as the*
> *stars of the heavens, and all this land that*
> *I have spoken of will I give to your seed, and*
> *they shall inherit it forever. Then the Lord*
> *turned from the evil which He had thought*
> *to do to His people.* (verses 11-14)

Notice that Moses put God in remembrance of the promise He had given to Abraham and his seed. Just like Daniel, he based his petition on God's Word. Even so, it wasn't simply God's Word that saved the Israelites, it was God's Word *in the mouth of a man.*

That point becomes even more clear through an incident recorded in Numbers 14. There, we see the Israelites once again in such stubborn rebellion and unbelief they were wanting to stone Joshua and Caleb for telling them

God would take them victoriously into the Promised Land.

And the Lord said to Moses, How long will
this people provoke...Me? And how long will
it be before they believe Me...for all the signs
which I have performed among them? I will
smite them with pestilence and disinherit
them, and will make of you [Moses] a
nation greater and mightier than they.
But Moses said to the Lord...Pardon I pray
You, the iniquity of this people according
to the greatness of Your mercy and loving-
kindness, just as You have forgiven [them]
from Egypt until now. And the Lord said,
I have pardoned according to your word.
(verses 11-13, 19-20)

Read that last sentence again. God didn't say He would pardon according to His word, He said He would pardon according to *Moses' word.* God listened and changed the course of history because one man dared to speak.

Just think, Moses' relationship with God was based on the old covenant. The Bible says the new covenant we have is better! How much more influence do we have with God, seeing we have access to the throne of grace that Jesus won for us? How much greater heed will He give to our words when they are based on the covenant blood of God's own Son?

If we will just pray and use the divine leverage God has given us, there is no end to what we can accomplish for Him!

Settle Down on the Promise

One thing is sure, however. Before we can lift God's Word to Him in faith, we must first focus our own attention on it. We must do as the Lord instructs in Proverbs 4:20-21 KJV, "My son, attend to my words; incline thine ear unto my sayings. Let them not depart from thine eyes; keep them in the midst of thine heart."

We must turn the eyes of our heart away from the problem, away from the darkness of the current situation we are praying about, and fix them instead on what God has promised to do about that problem. Then we must keep them there until we have seen it coming to pass with the eyes of our heart. For then, and only then will we be able to believe we receive when we pray.

Jesus said it this way in Luke 11:34 KJV. "Your eye is the lamp of your body; when your eye...is sound and fulfilling its office, your whole body is full of light; but when it is not sound and is not fulfilling its office, your body is full of darkness." In other words, the way you act, speak, and pray will be determined by where you are looking. If you're looking at circumstances, you'll be filled with discouragement. If you're looking at the Word, you'll be filled with faith.

That's important to remember because often when you are praying for a person, the Lord may show you dark things. You may see, for example, the person is demonically oppressed or even possessed. At times, such revelations throw people off track in their prayers. They'll focus their attention on the darkness and get discouraged. Eventually, instead of praying, they end up on the phone gossiping about it.

But that's not what the Lord intends for us to do with the information He gives us. (And if we continue to behave that way, He'll stop revealing such things to us because we're untrustworthy.) He intends us to take the darkness and hold it up to the light of His Word. He expects us to have more confidence in His promise than any demon hell can dispatch. He expects us to say, "Darkness, you flee in Jesus' name! God's will *shall be done* in this person's life!"

Often our faith falters in those situations because we haven't taken the time to truly settle down on God's promise concerning them. Maybe we've read it and confessed it a few times, but we haven't firmly laid hold of it. So when the pressure comes, God's Word slips through our fingers like a greased pig.

What should you do in such cases? First, stop frantically making requests of God. (Remember, prayers not based on faith in the Word are a waste of time.) Then, start fellowshipping with Him and abiding in His Word about the situation. Spend more time seeking God and getting established on His answers in the Word than you do presenting the problem to Him. Meditate on that Word until it becomes bigger in your heart than any situation—bigger than any doubt the Devil can bring. And once established on that Word, do whatever it takes to continue holding onto it.

No Quick Fix

Sometimes getting settled down on the Word takes a long time. I remember one particular situation where I was praying for an individual who was very close to me. I was so emotionally involved in the outcome that at times the Devil would say to me, "You're so close to this situation, you won't be able to hear your heart and trust the Word. You won't be able to pray effectively."

So I would go to the Father and say, "Lord, You promised the Holy Spirit would help me pray and that He would guide me into all truth. So I'm trusting You to help me set my emotions aside and see Your truth in this situation."

After the situation was prayed through, I checked my diary and found that it had taken me eleven and a half hours of prayer just to get my heart settled on the Word. I didn't do it all at one time, of course. I just kept at it day after day, until I was so confident in God's promise I could just rest on it when I prayed, knowing His will would be done.

Sometimes we get in a hurry and don't want to take that kind of time. We want a fast answer, a quick fix, so we can get on with other things. But God isn't as interested in fast things as we are. He is more interested in getting them done according to His plan.

Some years ago, a friend of mine gave me a letter written by Dr. Lillian Yeomans. Dr. Yeomans was a great minister, as well as a deep person of prayer. Although she has been with the Lord many years now, the words she wrote to Irene, her friend and partner in prayer have encouraged me many times. (They were praying together for Rudy Vallee's salvation.)

Her words have reminded me again and again to settle down on God's Word when I pray. I trust they will do the same for you.

January 13, 1942

I cannot resist answering your letter, and enclosing a copy of one from Rudy to you, at once though I have no time to do it. I ought to be praying, but I ask God to let me pray all the time I write it. I know of a man who was a chef—at least, that is what people called him—but he was really a prayer. Miss Sisson told me about him. She said he was simply a prayer. He was particularly burdened about the Spanish American War and Sister S. believed that God gave America victory in answer to his petitions. If he was making fancy rolls, it was a prayer making them. She said they always turned out all right.

Rudy's letter is encouraging and we should rejoice over it as Elijah rejoiced over the cloud like a man's hand. He said in substance, "It's not going to stop with that. We are in for a deluge. Tell Ahab to get ready for it, that the rains stop him not." And the clouds grew blacker and blacker and there was wind and a GREAT RAIN. (1 Kings 18:44-46) It is coming. God abideth faithful. He cannot deny Himself. (2 Timothy 2:13) I give you these references so that you can look them up and read and read them. I am so glad that you are solidly founded on God's word in this prayer [for Rudy] but you need to settle down on it deeper, and deeper.

Always turn the light of the scripture on your prayer. The Bible is God Himself talking to you, revealing His will. For what are you praying? The salvation of a soul. For the salvation of which Christ died in unutterable agony on Calvary. What is God's will concerning it? "He is not willing that any should perish, but that all should come to repentance" (2 Peter 3:9 KJV). And we read in 1 John 5:14,15 KJV that "if we ask anything according to His will He heareth us. And if we know that He heareth us, whatever we ask, we know that WE HAVE THE PETITIONS THAT WE DESIRED OF HIM." We must call it done. God cannot lie. Nothing less than this is faith.

George Mueller prayed for one man for 52 years and told someone who asked him whether he had any doubts regarding the man's salvation replied that he was just as sure of it as if he had seen him before the Throne. The man was saved at Mueller's funeral

....I think that what you and I lack in prayer is patience. Oh, how those words in Hebrews 10:35-39 KJV help me. They fill my soul with heavenly music. "Cast not away...your confidence which hath great reward...Ye have need of patience...that ye might receive the promise. For yet a little while, and he shall come."

Just let us, you and I, be prayers. "Praying always"... God will answer if we are like the widow in Luke 18.

Let us pray more than ever. God has us here to pray in these awful days. When our prayers are ended He will come for us.

CHAPTER 17

Love Never Fails

new commandment I give unto you, that ye love one another; as I have loved you, that ye also love one another. By this shall men know ye are my disciples, if ye love one another. (John 13:34-35 KJV)

In addition to settling down on the promise of God, there is something else we must do to persevere in prayer. We must obey the one law that Jesus gave us—the law of love.

True prayer and love are inseparable. Galatians 5:6 tell us that *faith works by love.* And since prayer without faith is prayer without power—when we're not praying in love, we're not really praying at all.

What does it really mean to live a life of love? First Corinthians 13 gives us a very clear picture.

> *Love endures long and is patient and kind; love never is envious nor boils over with jealousy, is not boastful or vainglorious, does not*

*display itself haughtily. It is not conceited
(arrogant and inflated with pride); it is not
rude (unmannerly) and does not act unbe-
comingly. Love (God's love in us) does not
insist on its own rights or its own way, for it
is not self-seeking; it is not touchy or fretful or
resentful; it takes no account of the evil done
to it [it pays no attention to a suffered
wrong]. It does not rejoice at injustice and
unrighteousness, but rejoices when right and
truth prevail. Love bears up under anything
and everything that comes, is ever ready to
believe the best of every person, its hopes are
fadeless under all circumstances, and it
endures everything [without weakening].
Love never fails...*(verses 4-8)

That's a pretty tall order, isn't it? We could never fulfill
it in our own strength. But, thank God, we don't have to!
When we were born again, God put His own love inside us.
Romans 5:5 KJV says it "is shed abroad in our hearts by the
Holy Ghost which is given to us."

Love Will Move You to Pray

If you will yield to the love of God within you, it will
be a compelling force in your life. It will stir your heart. It
will cause you to identify with people. It will help you see
their needs and reach out to the Father in their behalf.

That's what it did in the life of Jesus. Matthew 9:35-38
says:

*And Jesus went about all the cities and vil-
lages, teaching in their synagogues and pro-
claiming the good news (the Gospel) of the
kingdom and curing all kinds of disease
and every weakness and infirmity. When He
saw the throngs, He was moved with pity*

and sympathy for them, because they were bewildered (harassed and distressed and dejected and helpless), like sheep without a shepherd. Then He said to His disciples, The harvest is indeed plentiful, but the laborers are few. So pray to the Lord of the harvest to force out and thrust laborers into His harvest.

When Jesus looked at the crowds of people who came to Him, He didn't look at them like most of us do. He didn't just see their clothes and their hairstyles and how they were acting. The Holy Spirit revealed to Him the condition of their hearts. He saw how desperately they needed help and guidance. And moved by the love of God, He said to His disciples, *Pray!*

The same thing will happen to us when the Holy Spirit reveals to us the hurt in people's lives. The love of God will rise up within us and compel us to pray.

Your Divine Safeguard

Once we've begun to pray, it is love that keeps us from getting into trouble.

"Trouble?" you say.

Oh, yes. Ask any pastor who has seen prayer groups in his church slip out of love and go awry; he will tell you just how much trouble they can bring!

You see, prayer conducts great power—more power than most of us even realize. However, wherever there is great power, there is also great danger. So it is necessary for precautions to be taken in handling it.

When I was a little girl, sometimes I would take a battery and touch it to my tongue. I liked to feel the spark of electricity it generated. I didn't have to worry about that battery hurting me because there was only a small amount of power in it. There was no great need for protection.

But if I went to an electrical power plant, I wouldn't be so casual about the voltage produced by the equipment there. In fact, I probably couldn't even get to it. I'd be stopped by locked gates and signs that read: DANGER. HIGH VOLTAGE. DO NOT ENTER WITHOUT PROPER EQUIPMENT. That's because without the proper safeguards, such power—which can be of so much benefit when conducted correctly—can be extremely destructive.

Love is your safeguard where prayer is concerned. It will keep you conducting the power properly. It will keep you from being drawn off into the Devil's territory and getting hurt.

Pride Goes Before a Fall

As we saw in 1 Corinthians 13:5, for example, love will keep you out of pride. I don't know why it seems these days when some people grow a little in prayer, they grow in pride too. Prayer doesn't qualify us as super-saints. Prayer is basic Christianity. It's just yielding to the Holy Spirit. Any believer with a willing heart can do it.

Even so, some people who pray get puffed up about it. They esteem themselves as more spiritual than others, thinking they can hear from God better than anybody else.

Do you know what the Bible says about that? It says, "Pride goeth before destruction, and an haughty spirit before a fall" (Proverbs 16:18 KJV). Pride is what cost the Devil his anointing and his access to the presence of God. Pride is what deceived him into thinking he could be like the Most High.

I'm telling you, pride can open you up to the silliest deceptions. It can make an absolute fool of you. But you won't fall prey to it if you'll walk in love.

When Ye Stand Praying—Forgive

Love will keep you from short-circuiting your prayers with unforgiveness too. You can pray the prayer of faith all day and all night but if you're praying it with unforgiveness in your heart, you might as well be whistling in the wind because those prayers aren't going anywhere.

That's why immediately following His teaching on the prayer of faith Jesus said, "When ye stand praying, forgive, if ye have ought against any: that your Father also which is in heaven may forgive you your trespasses. But if ye do not forgive, neither will your Father which is in heaven forgive your trespasses" (Mark 11:25-26 KJV).

Faith just won't work in an unforgiving heart.

Beware of Envy and Strife

Love will also keep you out of envy and strife. Those are two things every praying person must definitely avoid. For as James 3:16 KJV says, "Where envying and strife is, there is confusion and every evil work." Can you imagine trying to hear the still, small voice of the Holy Spirit telling you what to pray when your heart is filled with confusion? You can't do it. So you must determine to stay out of strife and yield to love no matter what the cost.

Some years ago when Mac and I were first getting started in ministry, there was a person who persecuted us terribly. She made false accusations against us. She told lies about us. I was very tempted to take offense, but I resisted the temptation because I knew only love could take all of us through the situation unharmed.

When I talked to the Lord about it, He told me to pray for her every single day for 15 minutes. "And when you pray," He said, "I want you to pray believing that by sowing that prayer, you will reap her love in return."

I'll be honest with you. I didn't want to do it. I could think of a lot of other ways I'd rather spend those 15 minutes. But I did it anyway and I'm so glad I did because as I prayed for her, the Spirit of God began to show me the demonic pressure that was coming against her and causing her to persecute us. It was far greater than the pressure we were feeling from the persecution itself.

Then the Lord showed me through the Word how people who persecute the Church end in destruction unless someone intercedes for them. That changed my whole perspective. Suddenly, instead of being concerned about the pain she was bringing on *us,* I became concerned about the pain and destruction the Devil was bringing on *her.* Compassion welled up within me and I wanted to pray and bring relief to her.

Love caused me to lay down my hurt feelings. It caused me to set aside the offense I was carrying against her and cry out to heaven on her behalf. It lifted me above the whole situation on the very wings of God.

Love Will Give You God's Perspective

In Matthew 10:38-39, Jesus said:

> *He who does not take up his cross and follow Me [cleave steadfastly to Me, conforming wholly to My example in living and, if need be, in dying also] is not worthy of Me. Whoever finds his [lower] life will lose it [the higher life], and whoever loses his [lower] life on My account will find it [the higher life].*

Love will lead you to lay down your life. It will lead you to deny yourself the things that are precious to your flesh; to die to your own feelings, rights and preferences. Love will even cause you to lay down your own point of view and take up God's perspective instead. It will enable you to hold onto someone in prayer and believe in their deliverance even when people tell you there is no way that person can ever be delivered.

A lady who was suffering from depression once told me her psychiatrist had given up on her 10 years ago. (I wanted to ask her why she was still going to him!) She may have looked like a hopeless case to that psychiatrist, but she didn't look like a hopeless case to Jesus. He never gives up on anybody.

It doesn't matter what the Devil does. It doesn't matter what kind of bondage he brings. Jesus still sees people through the promise of God. And He'll help you see them that way, too, if you'll let Him. He'll give you God's promise for someone, and then the love of God in your heart will cause you to hold onto that promise when nobody else would.

Love will keep you praying for that person when your own flesh is weary and your carnal nature wants to forget him and let him go. It will keep you believing the best, even when the situation seems beyond hope.

God's love in you will get you started in prayer. It will keep you safely conducting prayer's power. And it will give you the divine energy to pray all the way through to victory. For "love never fails" (1 Corinthians 13:8).

INDEX